LORD!
WHY IS
MY CHILD
A REBEL?

Parents and Kids in Crisis

Jacob Aranza

HUNTINGTON HOUSE, INC.

Huntington House Publishers
P.O. Box 53788, Lafayette, Louisiana 70505

Library of Congress Card Number 90-80223
ISBN 0-910311-62-5

Cover design by Hanson Design, Tyler, Texas

Typesetting by Times Graphics, Lafayette, Louisiana

Printed in Colombia

Dedication

To Brian and Louise Baudoin, the most godly parents I have ever had the privilege of knowing. Thank you for your counsel, love, prayer, patience and most of all for your daughter, Michelle. May we strive to be the parents to our children that you have been to yours.

Acknowledgements

The author would like to express his deepest thanks to John Offutt for his contribution of Tips for Parents. The author also thanks Jan Rogers for her perseverance and patience.

Table of Contents

1

A MOTHER'S CRY

Alice leaned over the kitchen counter feeling more lonely and rejected than she had ever felt in her entire life. Just moments earlier she had come face to face with every parent's nightmare. Her head was numb and tingling. She knew it had just happened, but she could not bring herself to believe it. Only three days earlier, she had been mentally patting herself on the back for being one of the best mothers she knew, always concerned and extremely devoted to God and to her children. Why had this happened to her? Alice and her husband had disagreed on how to discipline the children before, but even he could not believe this.

The day began like so many before it. Up at 6:30 a.m. for a breakfast of eggs, toast and a quick cup of coffee, then off to work. Everything seemed typical, even the same problems with her grumpy boss Mr. Sellers. When the clock finally signaled 5:30, it was a welcomed sight. While driving home Alice caught a glimpse of herself in the rear-view mirror and thought of the way she was aging. Yes, she was aging she calmly acknowledged, but quickly reassured herself that she looked younger than many women her age. As she pulled into the drive, she congratulated herself on a well-manicured yard. Each azalea and petunia had been carefully planted with her own hands. Alice was proud of the green thumb she had developed so painfully.

As she walked in the front door, her 16-year-old daughter JoAnn was preparing to head out for the evening. JoAnn's attractive figure and beautiful long brown hair assured she never lacked attention from the male population. Like most Friday nights since her sixteenth birthday, JoAnn was going out for an evening on the town. "And just where do you think you are going young lady?" blurted Alice. "Now don't start Mom," JoAnn replied, "I told you last week that I had a date tonight." "You most certainly did not," responded Alice. JoAnn turned and headed for the door; Alice was close behind. "You are not going anywhere tonight until you get permission from me," Alice pronounced boldly as she grabbed JoAnn by the arm, just before she reached the front door. "I am too," declared JoAnn, "and you can't stop me." Shocked by JoAnn's response, before she even realized what she had done, Alice drew back her arm and slapped JoAnn across the face. At that moment, what seemed like years of pent up frustration exploded from JoAnn. She began swinging at Alice. The first blow that struck Alice drove her to the floor. Alice covered her face as an avalanche of blows struck her head. When JoAnn finally stopped, a throbbing numbness settled over Alice's body. Grabbing the arm of the couch just above her head, Alice pulled herself up and stumbled to the kitchen counter. The front door slammed behind JoAnn as she ran toward her date's car. "Dear God," Alice whispered, "what have I done?" Alice's mind drifted back to childhood. Remembering the time she was spanked for something her younger brother had done. It just didn't seem fair or right. Why me she thought, looking down at the counter through her tears. Alice, like many parents, had just been devastated by one she loved so much. Her scars, both emotional and physical, may take years to go away. Just because some scars don't show, the pain is no less overwhelming. Even though your scars may be different, the cry remains the same; Lord, why ....

2
Daddy Boy

ONE of the greatest joys of my life is a little fellow I call "Daddy Boy."

He's 3-feet, 4-inches tall, with chocolate brown eyes and beautiful straight brown hair.

He is really my son, Jacob, Jr., but he thinks his real name is "Daddy Boy" — and he likes it. And by the way, he is more important to me than life itself.

Now you may be wondering how on earth my wife Michelle and I began calling him "Daddy Boy."

Well, here's how it all came about.

When Michelle first became pregnant I was happy but just didn't get too excited about it.

One day Michelle said to me, "Honey, you're not all that excited about this baby, are you?"

"I am too," I replied.

"No, you're not! And this baby knows it," she said, "And if he doesn't, when he grows up, I'm going to tell him!"

But with the passing of time I really did get excited about the baby and with the idea of becoming a father. I even went with Michelle to LaMaze classes to learn childbirth breath-

4

ing techniques. I thought I had been breathing properly for 23 years, but now I had to help Michelle breathe with special huffs and puffs to cut down on the labor pain during delivery.

LaMaze would have been a lot of fun, but the night the baby came I was breathing so hard helping Michelle that I hyperventilated and almost passed out right there in the delivery room!

Jacob Junior was born at 3:14 on a Sunday morning, and I was so thrilled I was beside myself.

After spending some time with Michelle and our new baby, I left the hospital, slept a few hours, then drove to Houston, Texas, 200 miles away, where I was scheduled to speak that Sunday evening.

After the meeting in Houston, I went to Cincinnati, Ohio, for more meetings and by the time I was home again my little boy was 3-weeks-old.

Since my ministry often took me away for several weeks at a time, one day Michelle said to me, "Jacob, as much as you're gone, little Jacob is going to be a mama's boy."

"No way," I replied. "I was a daddy's boy and he's going to be a daddy's boy."

"How are you going to work that?" Michelle asked. "You're gone all the time."

"It's easy," I said. "I'm going to brainwash him."

So every time I came home from a trip, I would hold little Jacob in my arms, put my lips right beside his ear and say, "You're daddy's boy, daddy's boy, daddy's boy, daddy's boy..." for about 30 minutes every day.

Naturally, when he was able to talk and someone asked him, "Whose boy are you?" he replied, "I'm daddy boy."

Then a very interesting thing happened — he began to think that Daddy Boy was his real name and that it was my name also. He distinguished between the two of us by calling himself "Little Daddy-Boy" and me, "Big Ol' Daddy-Boy."

When Daddy Boy was 2-years-old, I came home from a speaking engagement and said to him, "I think you and I should go somewhere and eat. What do you want to eat?"

"I want some Mexican food," he said, being a good little Mexican boy.

So we drove to the city and found a Mexican restaurant.

He sat up in his seat happily dipping chips into salsa, just like a good little Mexican boy should.

Between bites he looked over at me and said, "Aren't we having a beautiful time, Big Ol' Daddy Boy?"

"Yes, son, we are having a beautiful time," I answered.

On the way home, he reached over from his car seat and put his hand around my arm as best he could and said, "I like you, Big Ol' Daddy Boy!"

I smiled and said, "I like you, too, Little Daddy Boy."

Only a parent can understand how times like these can warm your heart, fill you with joy, and make you say, "Thank you, Lord, for giving us this little fellow."

Little Daddy Boy is five years old now. Michelle and I have poured our lives into him. He can count in both English and Spanish, and he's beginning to speak in both languages.

When you ask him what he's going to do when he grows up, he says, "Preach the Gospel." If you ask him what he'll tell people when he preaches the Gospel, he says, "Repent and be saved!"

This is our wonderful little boy — God's precious gift to Michelle and me. We've had the privilege of staying up with him at night when he was sick. We've held him in our arms and walked the floor praying for God to touch him and take away some childhood sickness. We've changed his diapers and kissed his boo-boos when he's fallen down and hurt himself. We've told him about Jesus and how much He loves him, and we've told him that we love him more than anything in the world.

Yet one of the most frightening possibilities in all of life is that in the years to come, perhaps when he's a teenager or in his twenties, little Daddy Boy would get right up in my face and say to me, "I hate you. Leave me alone old man. I don't ever want to see you again. I don't need you and I don't need Mom. I wish you were dead!"

Then, with a broken heart, I would cry out to God in the midst of all my pain, "Lord, why is my child a rebel?"

The scenario I have described for you is more than a remote possibility, for there is a raging epidemic of teenage rebellion sweeping across our land, engulfing hundreds of thousands of families.

Statistics concerning runaways, young people using drugs and alcohol, teenage pregnancies, and teenage suicide don't tell the whole story, because when a teenager wanders off into rebellion it also creates a private hell for his parents.

Let me tell you about Laura. I first met Laura's parents when they came to see me in my office. They were deeply concerned about their daughter and wanted to talk to me about her. I motioned for them to sit down and we began to get acquainted. To my surprise they were much younger than I first guessed. Grief had etched deep lines on their faces.

First the father, then the mother, poured out their story. So much unhappiness over their Laura, and it came so unexpectedly into their lives!

Just the year before, Laura had been the joy of their lives. She had openly confessed a great desire to live a godly life.

"Everything was going just great," her father said. "Then it started: first the clothes, next the music, followed by a wild hairdo, and then her weird-looking friends."

"The last two days have been a nightmare!" her mother interjected. "She ran away. For two whole days and nights we didn't know where she was or what she was doing—or even if she was alive," Laura's mother said, twisting a handkerchief tightly in her hands.

The father resumed the account with, "Finally she showed up at home—no explanations, nothing. She won't even talk to us."

I just looked at this mother and father, their shoulders rounded with grief and helplessness.

Just then the door flung open and Laura strode into the room. She was a 16-year-old who, in spite of a punk haircut rising in multicolored spikes and a makeup job that would provoke Boy George to jealousy, could not hide a delicate hint of natural beauty. I offered her a chair and she draped herself over it, glaring at me and her parents.

Her father continued, "We always sent her to a Christian school. She's been in an active church youth group. We pray together as a family. What have we done wrong?"

The question hung in the air, just like so many I had heard before. Just like the question asked by the mother of Don.

Like 50 percent of American youth, Don came from a broken home. His mother and father divorced before he crossed into adolescence. No sooner were his parents separated than Don's mother married another man who had been waiting in the wings.

During the next two years, Don's mother not only found a new life in her second marriage, but she became a Christian and told Don she was different.

As she came to know more about Christ and his teachings, she could see the many mistakes she had made in her previous marriage, and in the way she had raised Don. She was forgiven by God, and it seemed as though tons of guilt were lifted from her.

But what about Don? Could the years of wrong be undone for him—ever?

Don began to resist the changes in his mother. He resented his stepfather trying to take the place of his real father. And his radically changed mother was so wrapped up in her new life that Don soon began to feel left out.

He expressed his hurt in any way he could. One day it would be a hovering quiet depression; the next day he would storm about in a violent rage like a caged wildcat.

Before his eighteenth birthday, Don had bounced back and forth between his mother and his natural father at least a dozen times. He seldom let his emotional guard down, even when his stepdad tried to show genuine love and concern.

The final conflict came right after Don graduated from high school. Fed up with his rebellion, Don's parents kicked him out. For Don, it was the final confirmation of what he had been feeling for years. He was left out and alone, where he felt he had been all along.

Then there was Sarah.

Sarah's mother is absolutely the sweetest mother I have ever met. She told me that her Sarah had been a model child: never rebellious, never disobedient, always the perfect helper around the house. She would even do house-cleaning chores without being asked.

Sarah's father had been in professional sports and prided himself on being a man's man. That attitude allowed little room for expressions of affection toward his daughter.

Unlike Laura and Don, though, Sarah's rebellion was hidden. She started stashing a fifth of whiskey beneath her mattress. It was her companion and object of affection.

Stowed carefully in her locker at school, like a prized jewel, was another bottle of liquor. Although her parents were still in the dark, Sarah's classmates knew her as the class drunk. She was often on a drunken trip before the second period bell rang at 9 a.m.

The mask Sarah wore at home hid the horror of her awful bondage.

I'll never forget the day that mask came down. I felt a sharp pain as I watched confusion and grief sweep over her mother's face. Her mother's cry was the same as the parents of Laura and Don. It is the same pain-ridden lament coming from the hearts and lips of millions of parents today—Lord, why is my child a rebel?

I have heard that question during 10 years of sharing and counseling with parents who have searched the Bible for answers.

You may already have experienced some kind of open rebellion from a child—a child you raised and nurtured. The same child who has brought such tremendous joy can bring equally terrible pain to your heart. You may already have experienced this as a cruel reality.

You may be crying out to God, asking Him, "What have I done wrong? Oh God, why is my child a rebel? Didn't I take him to Sunday school? Haven't I been a good parent? I prayed with him. We did the best we could. Why, Lord?"

This book is an attempt to answer these questions. It isn't a list of pat, simple formulas—that would be like offering a band-aid to someone who is bleeding to death. Instead, I have attempted to share direct, practical principles found in the Scriptures and in the experiences of other godly parents who have felt the same heartache you may be feeling.

This isn't a book of condemnation, either. I want God's Word to set you free as you apply these principles. The Lord knows your pain, and He has the answers you are seeking. He has great hope for you and your child.

The names and some of the details of individuals' stories have been changed to protect family privacy.

3

THERE'S A WAR ON!

IF we are really listening to God's spirit, we will hear that He is giving us a message for our generation. It is a message that has not changed for thousands of years, yet the Holy Spirit's emphasis will be the answer to the heart-cry of people today.

Martin Luther once said, "If I profess with loudest voice and clearest exposition every portion of the truth of God except precisely that little point which the world and the devil are at that moment attacking, I am not confessing Christ, however boldly I may be professing Christ."

The Old Testament tells us about a group of men called the sons of Issachar. In 1 Chron. 12:32, it says these men understood their times and knew what God's people should do.

Like the sons of Issachar, we must understand our times. Above all, parents need to comprehend the problems our youth are confronting.

Satan is engaging in the greatest attack on the home in history. The first institution God established was the home, so Satan has always sought to destroy it. But his present onslaught is building in strength and fierceness. We desperately need to see what Satan is doing and learn how to combat

11

him in our families.

What do you think the greatest problem among young people is today? Is it drugs? Is it promiscuous sex? Is it rebellion? None of these is the real problem. The heart of the battle is Satan's attack on the home itself. A victory for Satan in the home will doom our entire society.

The home is to society what the force of gravity is to the earth. Without it, everything is flung off into space with nothing to keep things anchored. When the enemy moves in and begins to destroy the family, society descends into chaos.

Let's take a look at what is happening.

Did you know that in the United States, one out of every four homes has incest in it? [1] Look down your street and think about that.

Child abuse has tripled over a 10-year-period. More than two million child abuse cases were reported in 1986 and 1,100 children in the U.S. died from neglect or child abuse in 1987. [2]

We have become aware of the plague of child abuse in our country, but did you know that in one out of every 20 homes there is parent abuse? [3] That is, some children are literally physically hitting their mothers or fathers.

As long as our country seeks answers in humanism, (putting man at the center of the universe rather than God), we are going to continue a moral, social, and economic decline. A number of countries in western Europe and in the Communist bloc are a few years ahead of us on this destructive path.

For an example of social decline in the West, we should look to Sweden. Sweden has a higher standard of living than the United States; it is second only to the world's richest oil sheikdom, Kuwait, in its per capita income. [4] Sweden has no poor people at all, though with an 80 percent tax for anyone with an income of $46,000 and a 23.4 percent sales tax, there aren't many rich people either.

This Scandinavian country has a very humanistic perspective and has tackled its social problems accordingly. For instance, they had a problem with incest, so a few years ago they legalized incest. Now it's not a problem anymore. It's legal for consenting children over a certain age to have sex with their parents.

When the Swedes approached the problem of child abuse without understanding God's principles of discipline for children, they went to the extreme. In July 1979, they passed a law making it illegal for parents to spank their children. Of course, if you do not discipline children, another problem arises. Your children begin to despise you. So Sweden's next move was to make it legal for children to divorce their parents. This law is already in effect in Australia. [5]

This is happening in Sweden today, and it could happen here tomorrow if we fail to understand God's principles for the home. By the way, Sweden has one of the highest rates of suicide in the world. They are proving that you cannot solve the problems of man outside of God. They have failed to understand that God's first establishment is the home and, when it goes, everything else goes.

If the family is God's foundation for society, then the relationship between husband and wife is its cornerstone. If we are to understand the problems of young people today, we must first look at the problems of the parents themselves. At the root of many family conflicts are unseen spiritual forces. These invisible enemies described in Eph. 6:12 are out to destroy homes and to turn husbands against wives and wives against husbands.

Consider some of the arguments you've had with your spouse lately. Didn't they start over the tiniest things? Sometimes I have dealt with people who have real violence in their home. I've asked them what happened and by the time they reconstruct it, they find out it started over some stupid little nothing. "It was my wife." "It was my husband." "He said this." "She said that." But do you know who was behind it all? Satan.

Wives, you must learn that your husbands are not your enemies. Husbands, you must learn that your wives are not your enemies. Husbands and wives, you must learn that you children are not your enemies. Teenagers, you must learn that your parents are not your enemies.

Satan is your enemy! He is the one who seeks to destroy you!

I have learned as a husband and as a counselor that I am not immune from these attacks. Satan leaves me alone until 30 minutes before we leave for Sunday services, then some little spark is set to an invisible fuse. By the time we get there, my wife and I are doing everything but choking each other. Of course, you have to put up a front and act like nothing has happened and go into church and talk about how good God is. What hypocrisy! In times like that, nothing of real spiritual importance takes place, because God only honors sincerity and honesty.

If we are honest with one another, we will admit that we are struggling. We all have problems and we all face that unseen enemy who seeks to destroy our homes.

Recently a major denomination conducted a poll to see what happens to their children when they graduate from high school. They discovered that 89 percent leave the church, with only 30 percent of them returning in their lifetimes. [6]

Satan's battleground today is the home, and that is where we have to face him. That's where we have to have prayer and Bible study; that's where instruction has to begin.

I hear people making such a fuss over the fact that we can't pray in the schools anymore. But I'm a lot more concerned about the lack of prayer in our homes. If we don't even pray at home, why should it bother us if we can't pray in school? Stop signing petitions to get prayer back in school if you're not even praying at home.

Crime statistics tell us that about 300 parents a year are killed by their children and that 31 percent of all violent crimes are committed by kids under the age of 18. [7]

I recently picked up a copy of *USA Today* and read about the minors on death row around the country. One, age 15, killed both of his parents. Another, a 17-year-old, raped and killed a nun. In nearly 30 years, from 1950 to 1979, crimes committed by youths jumped 11,000 percent in an explosion of violence. [8]

Parents today feel helpless. The attack on their children is coming from every area: television, music, kids at school, fashion, drugs, and alcohol. Who can parents trust, as they read of principals, teachers, police and firemen, scoutmasters, even clergymen being charged with child molestation? No wonder parents feel overwhelmed.

Why are these things happening? Is it because young people are worse than ever before? Do you believe that somehow, mysteriously, in the last 20 years, young people have degenerated to the worst depths in history?

Let me give you one older person's opinion and see if his words describe any of the kids you know:

> Our youth today love luxury, they have bad manners, contempt for authority, and disrespect for older people. Children are today's tyrants. They no longer rise when elders enter the room, they contradict their parents, chatter before visitors, gobble down their food, and tyrannize their teachers. [9]

Socrates wrote that 500 years before Christ.

I don't believe that children are any worse today than in past generations. But never in history have young people been exposed to the influences they are exposed to today.

There is a war against innocence in our society. When is the last time you saw somebody blush? That's a rare disorder that used to exist about 30 years ago. People don't do it anymore. Do you know why? Because nothing shocks us.

If you are old enough to remember when the Beatles first came to America, you'll remember how parents went crazy.

"What's wrong with those guys?" they demanded.

"Look at their hair! Listen to that music!"

15

That's just one indication of how far and how fast we have come. If rock groups today looked like the Beatles did then, parents would pack a picnic lunch and send their kids to the concerts.

A few months ago, I went to a concert of a certain heavy metal group. In the audience young people were grabbing each other, sexually molesting strangers. Girls were taking off their bras and panties and throwing them to the entertainers on stage. The members of the band bragged during the performance about who they had sex with that afternoon, describing the proportions of their bodies and how many times they had orgasms. I watched, grieved, as 10, 11, and 12-year-olds in that audience ate up every word and every indecent action. What I saw that night could never have taken place in our country 20 short years ago.

The enemy has come in like a flood and has declared war on innocence. He wants to pollute your children with the same trash he has used to corrupt adults.

I was talking to a man recently who was not a believer. He was quite liberal in his views as he explained to me why he was not a Christian. But he made a comment that really struck me.

"I know when we lost control," he said. "It was after World War II. The men came back and decided they were going to give their children what they never had. The problem was, they didn't give them what they did have—respect for authority, a good spanking when they needed one, and a good healthy no when they needed to hear it."

James Dobson, one of America's foremost Christian psychologists, has said it takes a steady hand to handle a full cup. [10]

Many of us have given our children a full cup of material things that they could not handle. They have dropped it and we wonder why. We must adopt the attitude of the sons of Issachar who understood the times they lived in and knew what to do. In many ways, the generation of kids today are

16

unlike any before. Only as we understand this will we be truly prepared to help them.

4

KIDS TODAY
ARE DIFFERENT

SEVERAL phenomena make today's generation of kids different. I'll try to explain them as well as I can. The six observations which follow can help us to understand the special problems facing children today.

Kids Today Have Been Raised By the Media

This is the first generation that has had total media exposure. Young people cannot remember a time without television. They were reared with TV as babysitter, companion, and comfort. Is it any wonder that when you try to turn it off they get upset? Why should they listen to you? They have spent many more hours listening to television than listening to you. Why should they start now?

Some studies have shown that American children between the ages of six and 16 spend an average of 20 to 24 hours a week watching television.[11] If a child lives to be 80, and that viewing rate continues throughout his life, he will have spent approximately eight to 10 years of his life watching television. Ironically, statistics tell us that parents spend less than two minutes a day communicating with their children; the average father spends only 37 seconds a day talking with his son. [12]

Studies show that American parents spend less time with their children than those in most other countries in the world. Even in Russia, where both parents work and where children spend a great deal of time in child care facilities, emotional ties between children and parents are stronger and time spent together considerably greater than in the U.S. [13]

What about schools? Aren't they the major influence on our children? By the time the average young person graduates from high school, he has spent 11,000 hours in the classroom. Yet that same young person has been exposed to almost 10,000 hours of television. When you add that to movies attended and music listened to, it totals 32,000 hours. [14]

How about the church? There the actual input is even smaller. Children raised in good Christian homes only receive an average of two hours a week in spiritual training.

The mass media are training our children. Is it any wonder kids want to live out the lives they have seen on TV?

What would you do if someone came into your home and began to talk to you and your child like this: "Did you know the lady next door is having an affair with the man across the street? They are in the bedroom right now and they left the windowshade up. Come over here to the window—we can watch them having sex!"

How would you react if a person walked into your house and talked like that to your child? You would be furious, wouldn't you? And yet when television brings the same story into our home and unfolds it in front of our children's eyes, it doesn't bother us.

If we sit there and drink it in with them, it doesn't do any good to say, "Now don't you live like that. Just because I enjoy

19

this on TV doesn't mean I like it in real life." Don't forget: If we tolerate such things while our children are under our influence, they may well assume we endorse it.

Kids Today Fear They Have No Future

When the first atomic bomb was dropped on Japan in 1945, the shadow of its mushroom cloud extended over every baby born since then. More and more young people believe nuclear war is inevitable. In a TIME magazine poll, 32 percent of young Americans polled said their future would be affected by nuclear war. Sixty percent felt they would have no future at all.[15]

Our motivation for living is based on what we believe about the future. Is it any wonder most say, "Let's eat, drink and party because we're all going to be dead tomorrow"?

A nuclear mushroom cloud isn't the only thing hanging over the heads of kids today. In 1970, children age five to 11 were asked to list their five major fears. They listed:

1. Animals
2. Dark rooms
3. High places
4. Loud noises
5. Strangers

But look at the results of a similar poll taken in 1984 which revealed the most common fears of children:

1. That my parents will get a divorce
2. Nuclear war
3. Pollution
4. Lung cancer
5. Crime.[16]

That's quite a change in 14 years. Has there ever been a

generation that has had to cope with as much fear and despair as the present one?

Kids Today Reach Physical Maturity at an Early Age

Girls and boys are becoming physically mature at an earlier age. In the 1800s, the average girl began her menstrual cycle at age 17. Today, the onset of puberty often comes at age 12 1/2. [17]

Not only are children maturing physically faster, they are accumulating knowledge faster. Perhaps you have watched your kids, tinkering happily with computers that stump you. Or you've seen them with lightning-quick reflexes at the controls of a video game moving so fast you can only see half of what's going on. You may conclude that children are smarter today than they used to be.

Kids are exposed to much more today and have a lot of information in their heads. But knowledge should not be confused with wisdom. Wisdom is knowing the difference between right and wrong and being able to choose what is right. Young people may be smarter and physically stronger today but they aren't as emotionally mature as you were at their age.

If you combine the earlier physical maturation of today's youth, the accumulation of knowledge without wisdom, and hours spent with sex-saturated television, videos, music, and movies, you have a moral hand grenade with the pin pulled. No wonder one American teenage girl becomes pregnant every 31 seconds. [18]

Kids Today Must Make Important Decisions at an Early Age

This generation is having to make major decisions earlier. One reason for that is divorce. Six, 7- and 8-year-olds are being forced to choose between their parents. Children are torn between the two people they love most. Often, families are so fragmented that the emotional weight of holding the family together falls on the shoulders of the kids.

One girl, Mary, recalled her parents' divorce. She was only 4-1/2 years old, but the lawyer put her on the witness stand and asked her, "Who do you want to live with?" [19]

Even in homes with happily married parents, media exposure is forcing more and more decisions to be made by children instead of by their parents. Kids have always been subject to peer pressure when it comes to clothes and entertainment. But now, with the skillful manipulation of the media, that pressure has been turned up 1,000 percent, bringing parents under the control of their children.

For instance, many kids feel they can't go to school unless they're wearing $100 worth of clothes with all the right labels. Look at the phenomenon of "501" jeans. They have replaced designer jeans as the hottest things going for young people to wear. How did that happen? The manufacturer, Levi-Strauss, went to the media with a cool, savvy advertising campaign aimed at kids which aired during the massive TV coverage of the Los Angeles Olympics. Now, many teens wouldn't be caught dead wearing anything else.

Jeans may not matter, but what should concern us is the way children are being conditioned to respond to marketing strategies determined by advertisers. This can be especially alarming when you realize that the entertainment and news media is controlled by a group of only 1,000 people and, according to a study of these media elite, 93 percent never attend church, more than half do not see adultery as wrong, a miniscule five percent believe homosexuality is wrong, and yet two out of three believe that entertainment should be used to reshape American society. [20]

22

Kids Today Suffer The Loss
Of Traditional Families

Most of us were raised in families where Dad went to work and Mom stayed home to take care of us. When we got off of the school bus, Mom was there to meet us, hear about what happened that day, and sit us down with a good snack before we did our homework.

Did you know that traditional kind of home has almost disappeared? Today, only 7.3 percent of our families have what used to be considered the American ideal. More than half the children under two years of age are warehoused 10 hours a day, six days a week in day care centers. Ten million children under the age of 10 come home from school every day to an empty house. [21]

Who is there to meet these kids when they turn the key, come in and throw their schoolbooks down? For many, it's not only television, but cable television. It's there to give them nudity, profanity, and raw violence. Is it any wonder that a recent study by the Catholic University of America found young people from two-income families routinely left unattended are more likely to engage in sex? Researchers at Indiana University found that 55 percent of junior high children 12 to 14 are now sexually active. [22]

As hard as pressures are on children with two working parents, it is even worse for those from homes ripped apart by divorce. The U.S. divorce rate has risen 700 percent in this century and continues to soar. If the divorce rate continues to increase as it has since 1960, in 19 short years there will not be one non-divorced family in America. [23]

A close, warm, sustained relationship with both parents has been shown to contribute most to the emotional development of a child. Yet more than one million children are involved in divorce cases each year, and half of all U.S. children under 18 have one or both parents not living in the same home. [24] Children from broken homes have what one

23

study cited as a "strikingly higher" incidence of emotional disorders.[25] They are more likely to suffer low motivation, low self-esteem, and are more susceptible to group pressure and juvenile delinquency.[26]

In a 5-year study of 60 divorced families by Wallerstein and Kelley in 1980, the following was found:

- The initial reaction of more than 90 percent of the children of divorced parents was an acute sense of shock, intense fears, and grieving which the children found overwhelming.

- Half the children feared being abandoned forever by the parent who left, (a realistic fear in the light of other studies that show that within three years of the divorce decree, 50 percent of the fathers never see their children). One-third of the children feared being abandoned by the remaining parent.

- Two-thirds of the children, especially the younger children, yearned for the absent parent—with "intensity we found profoundly moving." [27]

Kids Today Are Surrounded by Alcohol and Drugs

With so many hurting children is it any wonder kids begin to try things they don't have the wisdom to handle? When they come home to an empty house after school, who is there to keep them from tasting the wine and beer in the refrigerator?

Anything with more than 2-percent alcohol was in Bible times not considered wine but strong drink.[28] There are 74 Scriptures in the Old and New Testaments pointing out the dangers of alcohol, telling us to avoid strong drink, warning that violence, adultery, sorrow, contentions, and addiction are its results.[29] Would Jesus have disregarded such scriptural warnings?

You may not think there is anything wrong with an ounce of wine or beer; but there is definitely something wrong with an ounce of compromise. Whatever your children see you doing in moderation, they will be tempted to do in excess.

The problem begins with the first drink, social or otherwise. People often point to France and argue that French children are exposed to wine at an early age and taught to use alcohol with moderation. Yet France has one of the highest rates of alcoholism in the world. Definitions of alcoholism differ from country to country, but some estimate 15 percent of the adult population of France to be alcoholics.[30] France is second in the world in the rate of deaths from cirrhosis of the liver—a disease caused by alcoholism.

Alcohol remains the number one drug problem of our country. No matter how socially acceptable drinking is, you cannot call it safe and harmless.

Alcoholism among the young is rapidly escalating. America now has 3.3-million teenage alcoholics. Two years ago, 40 percent of the teens asked, said that they drank on a regular basis; a year ago 60 percent said that they did. It's gone up 20 percent in two years.[31] Why? Because alcohol is the most accepted drug in society.

Kids Today Don't Have Heros

Is it any wonder that with families disintegrating, the media bombarding youth with sexual messages, and schools teaching them that they are descended from monkeys, that there is no moral glue binding children to their families?

In a recent poll, young people were asked who their heroes were. For the first time ever, 51 percent of the young people said, "I have no hero, there is no one I look up to and admire."[32] No wonder kids are turning to Rambo, Prince, Madonna—anyone they can hold onto as a hero.

For many of us, sending our kids to school is like putting them into a moral jungle from eight in the morning until three in the afternoon. In 1940, public school administrators listed the major problems in public schools:

•Talking
•Chewing gum
•Running in the halls

A similar group in 1985 listed the major problems on their campus to be:

•Rape
•Robbery
•Assault [33]

Our kids are looking for someone to trust. They have seen government and religious leaders exposed for lying, immoral conduct, and outright crimes. Some of their teachers, city councilmen, and congressmen are openly homosexual. One-third of the girls and one-seventh of the boys have been sexually molested before they are 18 years old—usually by a member of their own family or another trusted authority figure. [34]

Yes, kids today are rebellious. This is one of the most rebellious generations in history but only because they have been hurt more than during any other generation.

Do you know what rebellion is? Rebellion is hurt that has been prolonged. When someone is hurt, their feelings progress from hurt to lack of forgiveness, to resentment, to bitterness, and finally to rebellion. No child simply wakes up one morning as a rebel.

Our kids are hurting. Why do you think they are dyeing their hair purple and green and sticking pins in their faces? They are looking for someone to tell them they are important, that they are noticed and accepted. If they don't find that at home, they will look for it in the streets.

What Do the Wounded Run To?

There are three escape routes for children in emotional pain. The first is withdrawal.

Parents say, "I don't understand! Johnny goes to his room, stays locked up there, gets on the phone or turns on the stereo. He never comes out, and never wants to talk to anyone."

Haven't you ever been hurt so badly that you wanted to get away from everything? Young people are withdrawing to their music, movies, comics, videos, and increasingly, into witchcraft and the occult.

Geraldo Rivera horrified the nation with his special on Satanism. Viewers watched as a handsome, gangly youth described how he and two other high school students bludg-eoned their friend to death as a sacrifice to Satan. A few weeks later, police made the grisly discovery of 13 bodies across the border from Brownsville, Texas. These were also victims of Satanic rituals. The cult was led by two attractive young people—one, a girl, was a college honors student.

Terrifying as these cases are, they are not isolated occur-rences. Increasing numbers of young people are escaping into the world of the occult. I counsel about 20 youngsters every week, and two things account for the bulk of their problems: depression and the influences of demonic cults.

The second refuge for hurting youth is even more common; it's drugs and alcohol. Young people from good homes, from small towns, from nice neighborhoods are increasingly seek-ing anything to numb their minds and emotions. They can't deal with the pain of living, so they turn to sniffing glue or gasoline, taking drugs or drinking alcohol—anything to "numb out."

The third refuge is the most tragic of them all: for increas-ing numbers of teenagers, the only option to life is suicide.

Among 15- to 19-year-olds, suicide has gone up 400 percent in the last 10 years. Every 90 minutes an American teenager kills himself. More young people committed suicide last year than have died from AIDS in all the years since that disease appeared.[35] We hear a great deal about combating the spread of AIDS, but suicide among teens is a greater epidemic.

To consider these alarming facts about our generation may be depressing, but there is hope. In the following chapters we will see that there are practical ways to combat all of these problems by applying principles based on the Word of God.

5
RECOGNIZING A REBEL

How do you tell the difference between a rebel and someone who has just blown it?

Let me tell you about two young people. One is a young man whom we'll call Peter. He sits dry-eyed through the most moving sermons at church, but at least he still goes with his parents. He doesn't openly defy them, but when they're not looking he is hanging out with friends, drinking, and laughing at everything he has been raised to believe in. One night recently his folks were horrified when he called them from the police station. He and some buddies had been picked up for drunk driving.

"It wasn't my fault, Dad," he pleaded over the phone. "I was just along for the ride—they were the ones who were drinking." His parents wanted to believe him, but they felt uneasy.

Another young person is Rachel. She also was raised in a Christian home, and to the relief of her parents, she never gave them a moment's worry. She made good grades, was active in their church youth group, and dated a nice young man—also from the church. She even spent a couple of weeks one summer on a short-term church mission to Mexico.

Rachel's parents were absolutely unprepared for what

happened next. There she was, standing in their kitchen looking very pale and scared, telling them she was pregnant! Suddenly, her parents weren't sure they had ever really known her.

In both of these instances, the parents needed to know how to react; with confrontation, or with forgiveness. It all depends on whether their child is a rebel or someone who has just blown it.

Let's look at the characteristics of a rebel, and differentiate between true rebellion and someone who has blown it. Both examples, as illustrated in the stories of Peter and Rachel, are also illustrated in the Bible in the story of Saul and David.

Saul was the one God chose to be the first king of His people. He searched the entire nation for the best leader and found Saul. God told the people, "Here is the king I have chosen for you." He was tall, strong, a warrior, a natural-born leader, and he was humble. According to the Lord, he was the best man for the job.

Saul began his reign well, relying on God's man, Samuel, for counsel. He united the people, was gracious to his detractors, and defeated the enemy of God's people in several stunning victories. If only Saul's story had ended there.

But Saul turned in his heart and became a rebel. You probably remember the story recorded in 1 Sam. 15. As we look at his example, the story gives us the classic characteristics of a rebel.

Saul was going into battle against the Amalekites. For reasons we aren't told in the passage, God wanted these people destroyed completely. He told Saul to spare none of the Amalekites—not even the livestock. Saul went into battle, defeated them, and killed most of the people. But he spared Agag the king and kept the best of the sheep and cattle alive.

When Samuel came to reprove him, Saul revealed the first sign of a rebel. He said, "Blessed are you of the Lord! I have carried out the command of the Lord!" (1 Sam.15:13, NASB) As they say in South Texas, that was a bold-faced lie!

Saul was in direct disobedience of the Lord and he knew it. He was a rebel, and like many rebels, he had become very good at covering up his sin. The second sign of a rebel is also shown in 1 Sam.15. Saul told Samuel, "I have carried out the Lord's command." That wasn't true—*he only obeyed in part*. Rebels never completely do what you ask them to do. They'll do 50 percent; they'll do 70 percent; they might even do 90 percent, but they never completely follow through. And this kind of conduct is not a one-time thing. For a rebel, it's a consistent attitude of life.

Samuel's response to Saul was almost funny. He said something like, "If you've obeyed God, what's all this 'baa-ing' and 'moo-ing' I hear?" There Saul stood, drowned out by the noise of all those fat cows and sheep (that God had instructed him to kill). And yet he was trying to tell Samuel that he had obeyed God.

Saul's next answer was another classic sign of a rebel. He was a blame-shifter. He told him that his people had done it—they were the ones who had kept the livestock alive. Who was king, anyway? Who had received the commandment of the Lord? Whose job was it to see that God's orders were carried out? It was Saul's responsibility, yet he tried to lay the blame on others.

Rebels are blame-shifters. It's never the rebel's fault. Whatever goes wrong, it's always someone else's fault. If a rebel does get caught doing something bad, he says everybody else was doing it, too. Rebels are always blame-shifters.

Another sign of a rebel is his unwillingness to give up his "rights." A rebel's concept of obeying God is giving up his wrongs but not his rights.

God didn't ask us to give up our wrongs. He didn't ask you to give up your smoking, drinking, and cursing. God asks us for our life, for your rights. If your feelings are hurt, give up your rights. A rebel hasn't surrendered, and he fights to preserve his rights.

Still another sign of a rebel is pride. Samuel saw this in

Saul. Samuel reminded Saul in 1 Sam. 15:17 of how he saw himself as small before God made him the leader of Israel. But things had changed. Now Saul was large in his own eyes and God was small.

If you want to get a rebel stirred up, just cross his pride. He will do anything he can to be sure that you and everyone else knows how he feels. Saul's real problem was his pride. He exalted his opinion over God's. God instructed him to kill everything, but Saul decided to kill almost everything. He thought his opinion was as good as God's.

Like all other rebels, Saul questioned authority. His attitude towards Samuel was, "Who do you think you are to tell me I'm wrong?" This is a major flaw in any rebel's character. He questions the authority of those over him.

When Saul claimed to have done what he did in order to make a sacrifice to God, Samuel replied, "Has the Lord as much pleasure in your burnt offerings and sacrifices as in your obedience? Obedience is far better than sacrifice. He is much more interested in your listening to him than in your offering the fat of rams to him." (1 Sam. 15:22, *The Living Bible*)

Pride leads the rebel to try and do something in his own strength, to make some sacrifice instead of obeying God.

Samuel went on to declare to Saul that rebellion was the same as witchcraft and stubbornness was iniquity and idolatry. When he told him that God had rejected him as king, Saul finally replied, "I have sinned!"

Rebels will always admit they're wrong in order to save themselves when they're cornered.

A guy named Harry was involved in drugs. He came to one of our meetings and spoke to me afterwards. "Man, you've got to pray for me, Jacob!" he begged. "Please, pray for me!" I said, "What's wrong, Harry?" "Man, I got busted big this time," he replied. "I just know I'm going to prison. Please pray that I won't go to prison."

I looked at him and said, "Harry, I'm not going to pray for

32

you." He said, "Why, man?" "Because you're not sorry for what you've done. You're just sorry you got caught."

A rebel is never sorry for what he's done. He's just sorry when he must bear the consequences of his bad choices.

For Saul, from that point on, God's Spirit and anointing were gone. God chose another—David—to become the leader of His people. A few years later, Saul's life and rebellion ended. Defeated in battle and fearing the humiliation of capture, Saul begged his armor-bearer to kill him. When the armor-bearer refused, Saul fell on his own sword.

But still death eluded him. We learn in the first chapter of 2 Samuel the rest of the story. A young man came along and found Saul, impaled but still alive. When Saul asked him to finish him off, the young man did.

Rejoicing in what he had done, the young man rushed to tell David (who was next in line to be king) what had happened. David asked, "Where are you from?" The young man responded, "I am an Amalekite."

Saul rebelled by refusing to kill every one of the Amalekites, and who killed him? An Amalekite. The moral of this story is: if a person doesn't get rid of his rebellious spirit, that spirit will get rid of him.

There are other well-known Amalekites in the Bible. Remember Haman in the Book of Esther who planned to kill all the Jews? He was an Amalekite. And King Herod, who tried to kill the infant Jesus by massacring every Jewish boy in Bethlehem under the age of two years? Herod was also a descendant of the Amalekites.

The Amalekites were used by the devil to come against God's plan for the birth of the Messiah. Thousands of innocents died because Saul in his pride and rebellion refused to obey God and utterly destroy the Amalekites. God saw what Saul could not see—the greater picture, hundreds of years into the future.

The Difference Between Rebellion and Someone Who Has Blown It

A mistake parents commonly make is to confuse someone who is in outright rebellion with someone who has blown it. Look at the biblical example of David, the king of Israel who followed the rebel Saul. David is a good example of someone who loved God but fell into sin. We can learn from God's treatment of David how to temper our judgement with our children when they sin.

David was a full-fledged hero. He was a Rambo. The crowds loved him and so did the women. What's more, God loved him, singling him out with some of the highest praise given a human being in the pages of His word. God said David was a man after His own heart (Acts 13:22). According to the record in Acts 13:36, David died, "after he had served his own generation by the will of God." You could hardly imagine this is the same man who committed adultery, tried to cover it up, and ended up a murderer.

You know the story told in 2 Sam. 11, leading up to David and Bathsheba's affair. David had retired from active service, sending others into battle while he remained home in Jerusalem. As so often happens when you rely on your past experience and take a spiritual vacation, David was ripe for temptation.

It came in a beautiful package. He was on the rooftop garden of his penthouse one day and looked down and saw a lovely woman—today we'd say she was a "fox". She was naked, taking her bath on a nearby roof. David gave in to lust. He decided he had to have Bathsheba. He found out that she was married to someone else—to one of his best officers, Uriah, away fighting the battle David was sitting out. But that didn't stop David. He sent for Bathsheba.

Even though Uriah was out risking his life for David and his country, David took Bathsheba and committed adultery. When she became pregnant, David sent for her husband to come home on R and R, hoping he would sleep with his wife and cover up David's adultery. It didn't work, Uriah was too good a man. He refused to enjoy the comforts of home and his wife—it was unfair, he said, when the men fighting with him were still out there on the front lines.

David knew it would be only a matter of weeks before Bathsheba's pregnancy began to show. He had to do something fast. Finally, he wrote a letter to his commanding general and asked Uriah to deliver it. Poor Uriah didn't know he as carrying his own death warrant. The letter instructed the commander to put Uriah into the worst of the battle and then pull back, leaving him stranded. It was murder just as surely as if David had wielded the sword that ended the life of one of the finest men to serve under him.

It doesn't sound like a man after God's own heart, does it? Yet David's story is not that of a rebel, but someone who has made serious errors in judgement.

David believed the devil's lie that he wouldn't get caught for his sin. He hurriedly married the widow Bathsheba and thought no one knew the truth. But God knew and He sent the prophet Nathan to confront David with his sin.

Nathan did it in a clever way, getting David to drop his guard until the point was driven home. He told David a story of a rich man with large herds who took the only pet lamb of a poor neighbor and slaughtered it to feed his guests. When David heard this he flew into a rage, demanding justice be delivered to such a black-hearted person. Nathan then stretched a bony finger toward the king and declared, "You are the one who has done this!"

The arrow found its mark. David immediately was repentant, crying out to God for mercy and forgiveness, confessing his sin.

Men always look on the surface; we cannot look on the heart as God does. That's why God tells us not to judge others. We don't have all the facts. Imagine if these two stories had broken recently in our modern news media. One leader has

35

been told by God to do something and he obeys 95 percent. He does *almost* everything God told him to do.

The second man, also in high public office, has just been caught in adultery and murder. Which would you say is more guilty? Which one should be thrown out of office? Who deserves a full-blown congressional investigation—the one who did 95 percent of what he was told to do or the adulterer/murderer?

Yet look what God did. He not only removed Saul from power, but He took His presence from him. Saul died away from God with no hope.

David was judged severely for his sin. First the baby conceived in immorality died. Then his son Absalom rebelled against him, almost taking his kingdom away. David sowed adultery and reaped the same thing—Absalom blatantly committed adultery with David's concubines on the roof of the palace for all to see.

Yet unlike Saul, David was forgiven and fully restored. He was even allowed to be the ancestor for the promised Messiah, Jesus. What was the difference between Saul, the rebel, and David, who had blown it?

David loved God with all of his heart; Saul didn't. God cares when someone blows it, but a person's response afterward is what makes the difference.

When he heard Nathan pronouncing judgment on him, the first thing David said was, "I have sinned against the Lord." David realized that the one whom he had hurt the most was God Himself. He was more concerned about that than the punishment God had pronounced through Nathan.

Contrast that with Saul's attitude when he was caught in sin. He denied his sin until he learned that God was going to take away his kingdom—then he tried to beg for forgiveness. He was totally unconcerned with the pain he had caused to the heart of God.

The second difference between a rebel and someone who has blown it is the willingness to accept responsibility for sin. Saul made excuses and shifted the blame to others; David said "I have sinned." He accepted full responsibility for his actions.

David loved truth and Saul didn't. When confronted, Saul tried to bluff his way out of a bad situation. He claimed to have obeyed the Lord. David, on the other hand, agreed with the truth of God even though it was against him.

If a person loves God, he will love truth. When I first became a Christian, the man who led me to the Lord gave me a New Testament. He asked later how I was enjoying it and I said I loved it! "I read two chapters last night," I told him. "Which chapters were they?" "Matthew and Mark," I replied. I didn't know yet that those were books, not chapters. I just knew I was starved for truth. The first week I was a Christian I read all the way through *Good News For Modern Man*. The more I read, the more I was set free and the more I wanted to be set free.

Someone who is truly born again is someone who loves truth, even when it hits him between the eyes.

David went straight to God to repent; Saul went to Samuel. When an individual sins, he has hurt God more than anyone else. He must go to Him in repentance, and then to the people he has hurt. But when a rebel is caught, he will try to go to people and get his position restored. He shows he is more interested in protecting himself and his reputation than in the consequences of his sin against God.

The greatest difference between David, the repentant sinner, and Saul, the rebel, was that David broke when confronted with his sin. His humility is recorded in the psalm he wrote afterward, Psalm 51:

O loving and kind God, have mercy. Have pity upon me and take away the awful stain of my transgressions. Oh, wash me, cleanse me from this guilt. Let me be pure again. For I admit my shameful deed— it haunts me day and night. It is against you and you alone I sinned, and did this terrible thing. You saw it all, and your sentence against me is just....
(The Living Bible)

Look at verse 16, and see how David learned the lesson Saul didn't:

You don't want penance; if you did, how gladly I would do it! You aren't interested in offerings burned before you on the altar. It is a broken spirit you want—remorse and penitence. A broken and a contrite heart, O God, you will not ignore.

David saw what Saul didn't; he couldn't cover up his disobedience with some religious act. He was willing to be humble before God.

Unlike man, God doesn't look on the surface of things. Even if you have sinned and greatly failed God, He looks at your heart to see if you are broken. That is the difference between a rebel and someone who is truly repentant. God is so kind that when a child is stubborn and hardhearted and doesn't come to Him to be broken, He allows circumstances to break him. As you continue to pray and respond correctly to your child, God will give him the opportunity to come in repentance and be broken before he is crushed by his rebellion.

38

6

THE REASONS
KIDS REBEL

REBELLION isn't manifested all at once. There are reasons for it. But we need to understand the difference between true rebellion, the assertiveness of young people who are learning about the world, and the resulting conflicts that are sometimes mistaken for rebellion.

Someone has pointed out that young people grow in three directions: they grow *up*, they grow *away* and they grow *toward*. Part of the process of growing away from Mom and Dad is a constructive kind of rebellion; this is really assertiveness, not rebellion. The teenager starts to try his wings, finding minor areas with which to disagree with his parents.

One child expert has noted that with this kind of healthy assertiveness, the young person, "cuts the apron strings but not the heart strings." If a teen has been raised in a loving, godly way and then allowed to grow away from his parents in some small ways, he will ultimately grow back towards them and his upbringing. But first, he must be allowed the space and freedom to become a unique individual; he should not remain under the protective wings of his parents all of the time.

One mistake Christian parents make is deciding that their child is a full-blown rebel when he makes one mistake. Even children who love Jesus are going to have their share of mistakes and make some bad decisions. You can't become a swimmer by reading a book, and you can't become an adult by listening to lectures on adulthood. The only way for a teenager to grow up is to stop relying on his parents and do things his way.

The wise parent allows a teenager to flex his intellectual and emotional muscles, knowing that some mistakes will be made. If a parent tries instead to shelter a teenager, he will end up with an immature adult who fears responsibility, is unable to make decisions, and who can't function without constant supervision.

Healthy Assertiveness and Open Rebellion: There Is A Difference

Assertiveness is positively constructive; it leads to maturity. On the other hand, rebellion leads to anarchy and destruction.

Assertiveness opens communication between parents and teenagers, allowing them to explore problems and understand one another's feelings. Rebellion closes communication between kids and their parents. Assertiveness is varied in expression and is an occasional thing.

One week, the young person fusses about clothes, the next week he disagrees with his folks about politics. But rebellion becomes specific and permanent; a "Cold War" settles down on the family, and parents fear to mention areas of disagreement for fear of permanently losing their child.

Rebellion leads a teen away from the broad road of life onto a narrow detour, while healthy assertiveness helps him understand life, his own role in the family, and so his role in a larger society.

Assertiveness makes an adult out of a child. Rebellion can make a criminal out of a son or daughter.

When parents allow their kids to go through a period of assertiveness without criticism, a teenager will know he is loved and has the freedom to be himself. [36]

You may have read the descriptions of true rebellion and find that they confirm your worst fears. Your son or your daughter is in rebellion against you and against God.

Before we discuss the reasons kids rebel, remember: God is always the God of the second chance. If you have made mistakes, if you have blown it as a parent, He does not condemn you.

Jesus said that you would know the truth and the truth would set you free. His truth doesn't come to push you further down into despair, but to show you the way out to true freedom.

A Mistake That Can Lead To Rebellion: Inconsistent Discipline at Home

Have you ever heard the "Golden Rule of Child Rearing," "Do as I say and not as I do?"

This maxim is usually accompanied by two standards of conduct: one inside the home and a different one in public. Kids watch as their parents do one thing at church and another at home. They watch as the careful piety of Sunday dissolves in the stress of everyday living. Worse yet, children see the injustice of being punished for behavior they see practiced by their own parents.

Someone wiser than I once said, "If you have good kids, for the first 18 years they do what you tell them to do. For the next 40 years they do what you've been doing." That might be terrifying to some of us; but it's true.

One thing is made plain in Scripture: You reap what you sow. Ninety-five percent of the time, children are only a reflection of what they see in their own homes. If there is inconsistency in your spiritual life, in your devotion, in the way you treat your kids and your spouse and the people around you, then in return you are going to reap the fruit of that inconsistency in your children.

Another type of inconsistency in discipline is to react differently to the same wrong-doing. One time your daughter does something unacceptable and you discipline her in a particular way; then another time, the same misdeed goes unchallenged. You are giving her mixed signals. She doesn't know what to expect from you and she becomes uncertain and wary.

Discipline should be consistent and prompt. If you let one thing after another go by unpunished, you are letting your own anger build up until it erupts.

My Dad used to let his anger accumulate. I would do some horrible thing for which I deserved 40 lashes and two years in prison. But you know what? Dad wouldn't do a thing. Then one day I would forget to put the garbage out and he'd beat the devil out of me.

Lack of consistent discipline allows you to hold malice in your heart against your children. The first goal of all discipline is reconciliation between you and your child. After your son does something wrong, fellowship with him cannot be restored until you have disciplined him.

It's the same between us and God. He disciplines us to draw us back to Himself. Everything God does is redemptive.

When you discipline your child, you are restoring your relationship. Even though he may not understand, you can hug him afterwards and tell him that you spanked him because you love him. Let him know that fellowship is restored and he is forgiven; his wrongdoing is in the past.

Both parents must share in the consistent and prompt discipline of kids. Let me give you an example of the wrong way to handle things.

It's Valentine's Day and Joe's wife Mary has decided to

surprise him when he gets home. The house is going to be neat and orderly and she's going to be gorgeous with every hair in place and her makeup just right. When Joe arrives, she will send their son to grandma's so that they can share a romantic candlelight dinner.

So she makes her preparations. At noon Mary puts curlers in her hair. She takes special care with her makeup. Dinner is already in the oven as she starts picking things up and cleaning the house.

There's a little 2-year-old boy who follows Mary where ever she goes, throwing everything she has picked up down on the floor again. Besides that, he drops a glass full of milk, shattering it on the kitchen floor. Before Mary can get that mess cleaned up, he has spilled a cup of orange juice on the living room carpet. She scrubs that up. It's a losing battle.

Then at 5:30 p.m. Joe walks in and says as he flings down his briefcase, "Hi honey, how are you?"

Here is a woman who used to look wonderful, but now her mascara is smudged, her hair is sticking out and she looks like Phyllis Diller. "Here," Mary screams, dragging the terrified 2-year-old behind her. "Take your son upstairs and spank him!"

Relieved that Mary isn't mad at him, Joe starts up the stairs to spank the child. About halfway up the stairs Joe realizes that he doesn't have anything against this poor petrified boy. What is this about, anyway?

So Joe spanks his son, as Mary insists he should. Joe feels bad about administering the punishment and he can offer no words of consolation to the young boy. After all, Joe isn't quite sure why he has been asked to discipline his son.

When Mary sees her son coming down the stairs crying, what does she do? She begins to cry and starts hugging the boy.

"Oh my baby," Mary wails, "You've got to forgive your father. He just gets carried away sometimes!"

What is the matter with this domestic scene? The husband

is an important person in a family. A child will view God, his Heavenly Father, in the same way he sees his earthly father.

If a wife doesn't exercise swift discipline when the child does something wrong, she forces that role entirely onto her husband. Then when he comes in, the children tend to think, "Here comes Frankenstein, ready to spank somebody!"

Not only will this wreck the relationship between a father and his child, but it will distort that child's view of God. It doesn't work for one parent to be Law and the other to be Grace.

Mothers, when your husband leaves the house, you are God's established authority in your home. When your son or your daughter does something wrong, you need to exercise swift, immediate discipline. And I mean discipline, not punishment; there is a difference. Punishment focuses on past misdeeds; discipline focuses on positive correction for the future.

The Scripture says, "Be sure your sins will find you out."

God says that as a positive statement. As you discipline your child properly, you are teaching him the principle of sowing and reaping. When he does something wrong, he receives the consequences of that wrong. When he makes bad choices, he reaps bad consequences. If you guard him from those consequences, you are teaching him that he won't reap what he sows.

Another goal of disciplining your child is to subdue his will. As he obeys you, he is learning to obey God. Kids desperately need to learn the pattern of becoming humble and submitting to the will of God, but they won't learn that lesson unless parents confront their will.

Parents usually have many misgivings about disciplining their children.

You may say, "My daughter said she would run away if I made her get rid of that music, those posters on the wall, and that guy she's dating. I just can't handle her running away!"

If the only reason your child is staying at home is because

you haven't laid down the law, then she has been gone for a long time. Your house is only her motel.

Parents also fear, "My child will hate me if I discipline him." Do you want to know the most bitter, resentful children I've ever met? The kids whose mothers and fathers failed to provide guidelines and discipline. Children who live in permissive homes have trouble believing their parents really care about them.

A wonderful young Christian lady told an eye-opening story about her son and his relationship to this stepfather.

She was divorced from the child's father when the boy was quite young. A few years later she heard the Gospel and became a wonderful Christian. After a time she met a fine young Christian man and they married.

However, her son had trouble understanding everything — the divorce, the remarriage, having a new stepdad, not seeing his real father. So he rebelled.

The mother did her very best to discipline the boy according to biblical principles. But as he grew older he would run away from her and she couldn't catch him.

The stepfather, who had been reluctant to administer too much discipline to the young boy, called him aside one day and said to him, "Your mother loves you, she cared for you when it was just the two of you and now you need to love and respect her. And if you don't I'm going to tear you up."

The boy blinked in disbelief but the warning had little effect on his attitude toward his mother. He still rebelled toward her authority and refused to obey her.

When the stepfather heard about it he took the boy, gave him a hard spanking, and told him he must respect his mother.

The mother said that a strange thing happened that night. The boy wanted to be close to his stepdad. He wanted to sit by him, to talk to him, to hug him.

That's what happens when a child finally learns somebody cares enough about him to discipline him. Later, during his college years, the boy became a youth director in a local church.

Young people need the security of boundaries. You owe your sons and daughters that protection. You're telling them: "Don't go past this line, son, or something bad will happen to you." Then if they do go out, cross that line, and something terrible happens, he will say, "Hey, Mom and Dad aren't as stupid as I thought they were!"

I've also heard a mother say, "What if I lose her? At least I know that she's here in my house, even though she's doing drugs and sleeping with boys. She won't come to church with us and she says ugly things to me and my husband, but I have her with me!"

There is a principle woven throughout the Word of God which says, whatever you compromise to keep you will eventually lose. In every single situation I've seen like this, the child never changes. Instead of keeping a child, by lowering their standards parents ensure they will lose that child.

Dudley Hall remarked that a parent who refuses to discipline his child reveals an improper attitude toward authority himself. He is sacrificing the welfare of his child on the altar of his own rebellion. [37]

Another thing you must remember: If you don't discipline your child, somebody else will. You have the opportunity to discipline him in love; if you fail to do so, the next authority he encounters will do it, but not out of love. His employer won't do it in love, and neither will the police or the penitentiary.

It is sometimes hard to discipline children. Parents always say, "It's going to hurt me more than it's going to hurt you."

The kid's reply is, "Yeah, but not in the same place!"

They will be parents themselves before they believe how much it hurts to be the one doing the discipline.

Scripture says that Jesus learned obedience through the things which he suffered. If He learned obedience through

46

suffering, how can we or our children learn it any other way? It doesn't matter if you are the one "dishing out" the discipline or the one receiving it; suffering must be endured.

> Now no discipline seems to be joyful for the present, but grievous: nevertheless, afterward it yields the peaceable fruit of righteousness to those who have been trained by it.

Heb.12:11

TIPS FOR PARENTS

•Sit down with your child and develop specific guidelines and boundaries for behavior.

•Make the consequences for violation of these guidelines very clear. Discuss them with your child so they have full understanding of what to expect .

•Be consistent with your child. Do not let your emotions destroy the purpose of what you are doing.

•Continue to stress your love for your child, even in the midst of a conflicting situation.

•Assure your child that your love is unconditional. You love them for who they are, and not what they do.

7

DISCIPLINING IN ANGER MAY LEAD TO REBELLION

DISCIPLINE your son while there is hope, but do not indulge your angry resentments by undue chastisements and set yourself to his ruin. (Prov. 19:18. A.V)

When I was small, my parents would stuff me and my five brothers and sisters into the back of a beat-up Chevrolet station wagon and we'd go on trips. You see, my Dad had this fantasy about "getting away from it all." Have you ever seen six little kids crammed into the back of a station wagon, with arms and legs hanging out the windows? I admit, we were a little bit on the wild side.

Dad tried to be an authoritarian person. As our noise and bickering increased, he would announce from the front, "Alright, we're going on this 8-hour trip. I want you all to sit back there and be quiet. I don't want you to talk, I don't want you to move, I don't want you to breathe until we get there!"

That was a challenge we took up. Six little faces were soon puffed out, each one holding his breath.

"Frank, do something!" Mom intervened. "They're not breathing!"

Soon, there would be a explosion of air—a sound like spluh-pfft! coming from my oldest brother's lips. It quickly spread through the back until we were all spluttering and giggling and poking one another. In seconds, pandemonium broke out, with small noses and mouths pressed against windows, and writhing bodies twisting and rolling.

"Marty!" Dad would fume, "Do something with your kids!"

After a few more miles and a lot more mischief from the back seat, Dad's fuse hit the main tank and he'd start swinging at us from the driver's seat, trying to hit the nearest ones. Of course, we boys would use our little sister as a shield, and none of his blows were landing anyway. And all of this was taking place while we were swerving and weaving down the road at 70 miles an hour!

"You all better shut up back there, or I'll...I'll...."

We'd scramble to the rear as far away from him as possible. "You...! Come here and let me hit you!" he'd yell, still gripping the steering wheel with one hand. "Come here!"

What did he expect us to do, lay our heads on the front seat so he could beat us?

We had it made, until Dad hit the brake and the car quickly slowed down beside the road. That's when we knew our party was over! We were all lined up—six little children beside the highway—and we finally got our long overdue spankings.

But isn't this typical? Don't most parents wait as long as possible before spanking their kids, finally spilling over in anger, out of control themselves?

Let me tell you what is wrong with disciplining in anger.

• It gives your children a bad view of authority.

• It shows them that discipline is not a loving thing, but something they should only fear.

• When you discipline in anger, you discipline too harshly, not justly and fairly. You're not in control of your emotions;

you're just spanking to relieve your frustration.

The pattern in many homes is for the father to respond in anger. The children learn to go to their mother when they have a problem, and she conspires with them to keep it from Dad. They're afraid to tell Dad, in case he flies off the handle.

Mothers, if you allow your kids to do this, you are subverting God's established authority in your home. Your children will not honor your husband.

Fathers, when your kid does something wrong and you hear about it, don't blow a fuse. If you need to discipline him, do it, but not in anger. If you are angry as you discipline, you are defeating the purpose of it.

Some have taken this to extremes that I believe are unhealthy, announcing to the child that he will be punished and then waiting for hours before delivering the spanking to make sure the parent "cools down" first.

I think that's cold-blooded, and it can wreck a kid's day. Discipline promptly, but count to 10 first, if you need to, to make sure your own emotions are in check. Explain to him what he has done wrong and why you have to spank him, then deliver the discipline in love.

I was watching a football game at a friend's house on a Saturday afternoon. I don't remember who the other team was, but the University of Texas was getting beaten by somebody.

All of a sudden, the smell of something burning filled the room. "What's that? Smells like burning tortillas!"

We both jumped up and ran into the kitchen, but we couldn't see anything burning.

"I think it's coming from the microwave," he said, and opened its door. Flames licked out, he grabbed the fire extinguisher and in a great blast of foam, put it out.

Just then one of his little girls came running into the room. She was crying in fear. "Oh, Daddy! I did it! I put a towel in there with some wax on it to melt it and I forgot about it. I'm so sorry, Daddy."

How do you think my friend reacted? Did he yell at his daughter, "Look at our microwave! You've ruined it!" Or, "Don't you know you could have burned the house down?" Or, "Why are you always so careless?" No. He didn't do that.

He crouched down on the kitchen floor, held her close to him in that smoky room and said, "Let me tell you something, honey. Microwave ovens can be replaced, but little girls can't be."

He told her in that one sentence that she was much more valuable to him than any material object could ever be.

Has your child heard that from you? If ever kids needed to hear how much you love them, they need to hear it now!

MORE WORDS ON DISCIPLINE...

Before Punishing Your Child...

•Make sure he is guilty of the deed.

•Be sure that the deed was done deliberately.

•If you are satisfied that he deserves disciplining, do it
right away. The sooner the penalty follows the misdeed,
the more effective it will be.

•The discipline given must be, as nearly as possible, the
kind that will produce repentance. Discipline should be
designed to bring about repentance. When a child does a
wrong thing, his conscience will tell him that he should
suffer for it. When a painful discipline is the natural
outcome of wrong conduct, then wrongdoing and suffering will be closely associated in his heart. You should
strengthen that conviction, so that in later life he will
know that if he lives and dies in sin, hell will be his
rightful end.

•Discipline, painful so that it will be remembered, should
be as short as the offense requires. This is in favor of the
occasional use of the rod. A little spanking will be remembered, but will not unnecessarily prolong the suffering.
(Prov. 23:13-14)

Be careful that you never harm your child's health. It's
possible to damage a child for life by too severe or too long-
lasting pain. However naughty, disobedient, or cruel children may act, justice must always be tempered with mercy.

When telling your child to obey you, avoid drawn out

conflicts. From some strange motive, there is occasionally a blank refusal by a child to obey a direct command. If he doesn't obey you in a reasonable amount of time, a prompt spanking is the best thing. The unfortunate course adopted by many parents is to try to force the child to obey, no matter how long it takes, and under such circumstances a regular battle between the wills of the parent and the child is a common experience.

The Habit of Obedience

• Begin early.

• Don't give too many commands.

• Be careful that every command given is within your child's ability to carry out.

• Be careful that your commands are good and lawful. Otherwise, how can you insist they obey you?

• Be careful that your commands are understood.

• Be sure to show your child, in a way that he can under stand, your strong disapproval of all disobedience.

You cannot pass disobedience by without notice. To do so is one of the surest methods of cursing your child for the present and for the future. In a very real sense, you are teaching him what his heavenly Father thinks of disobedience.

Things Parents Should Not Do

• You must never set things that are earthly and temporary above things that are heavenly and eternal. If you do, you can't complain if your children grow up to prefer the world and its charms, to following Christ in a life of holiness and self-denial.

• Don't fool yourself into believing that if your children are left to themselves, they will develop naturally into the godly, holy, self-sacrificing characters you desire—only to be disappointed if they turn out to be little devils, or grow up to be very much like big ones. (1 Sam. 3:13)

• Don't expect that children who possess any backbone of resolution and energy will be likely to submit their wills, first to their parents and then to God, without a great deal of patient and persevering effort on your part.

• Don't expect your children to be so naive that they won't see beneath the cloak of a false Christianity, especially if they find it in their own home.

• Don't expect your children to be any better in character and conduct than the example set for them—by you, by their friends, and by those with whom they spend time.

• Don't contaminate the love of beauty, which exists in the hearts of all children, through the destructive device of vanity.

• Don't fill the minds of your children with the idea of their supposed superiority, mental or otherwise, over their friends, schoolmates, and others.

• Don't allow your boys to think that they are more important than their sisters.

• Don't instill, or allow anyone else to instill into the hearts of your girls the idea that marriage is the chief end in life.

If you do, don't be surprised if they get engaged to the first empty-headed, useless fool they come across.

• Parents shouldn't discuss or argue about the conduct or character of their child while in the child's presence. If you do, don't be surprised if he takes sides with the father or mother, depending on whose ideas are the most favorable to his selfishness.

• Don't make favorites among your children, and then be surprised that those who are not the chosen ones should grow up with a sense of injustice festering in their hearts. This will likely cause them to forget all the love you have given them.

• Don't let your children have their own way or give them what they want merely for the sake of peace, or any other reason whatever, when it is opposed to your own judgment of what is best for them.

*The above was adapted from Chapters 22 and 23 of **Love, Marriage and Home** by General William Booth, published in 1902. It is used with the permission of **Last Days Newsletter**, Lindale, Texas.*

The Bible gives us much guidance regarding discipline. Here are some Scriptural references parents can study when pondering discipline problems at home.

Prov. 13:24	He who spares his rod of discipline hates his son, but he who loves him diligently disciplines and punishes him early.
Prov. 6:23	For the commandment is a lamp, and the whole teaching of the law is light, and reproofs of discipline are the way of life.
Prov. 3:12	For whom the Lord loves He corrects, even as a father corrects the son in whom he delights.
Prov. 29:15	The rod and reproof give wisdom, but a child left undisciplined brings his mother to shame.
Prov. 29:17	Correct your son, and he will give you rest: yes, he will give delight to your heart.
Prov. 23:13-14	Withhold not discipline for the child, for if you strike and punish him with the (reed like) rod, he will not die. You shall whip him with the rod and deliver his life from Sheol. [Hades, the place of the dead]
Prov. 22:15	Foolishness is bound up in the heart of a child, but the rod of discipline will drive it far from him.
Prov. 20:30	Blows that wound cleanse away evil, and strokes [for correction] reach to the innermost parts.
Prov. 19:18	Discipline your son in his early years while there is hope. If you don't you will ruin his life.

The Living Bible

TIPS FOR PARENTS

•Be careful not to react to your child in frustration or retaliation for a mistake or wrong-doing.

•If you are too angry with your child to respond under control, remove yourself from the situation until your composure can be regained.

•Be sure you know all of the facts before you make a judgement in haste.

•Discipline should always be given in the proper proportion to the offense. Do not allow yourself to over react.

8

LOVE MEANS ALWAYS HAVING TO SAY YOU'RE SORRY

Many parents believe they will lose the respect of their children if they admit they were wrong and apologize to them. Yet exactly the opposite is true.

When you apologize to your children, you show them that there is an authority above you that you honor: God. They will come to understand that you aren't on some kind of authority trip but are God's established authority in the home. The authority they respond to in you represents the highest and fairest authority of all: God Himself.

Children learn what they see acted out before them. Child educators call it "role modeling." You cannot avoid being a role model for your children. If you have shown them how to humble themselves and repent by doing it yourself, they will be more likely to follow your example when they do something wrong.

On the other hand, if you refuse to apologize when you are wrong, it leaves unresolved hurt in your child's life.

Let me borrow an example from Bill Gothard, one of America's premier Christian teachers.

Your little boy is six years old; you have decided to try and be with your children more, so you tell him on Sunday that next Saturday morning you're going to take him fishing.

Do you know what happens to a 6-year-old when you tell him on Sunday night that he is going to go fishing next Saturday? At 5:30 Monday morning, you wake to a clanging sound coming down the hall. What is that? It sounds something like a minnow bucket hitting the wall. Then you hear something that sounds like rods and reels scraping pictures off the wall. Your bedroom door opens and slams shut and you crack one eye open.

A little form is standing by your bed, burdened down with all the fishing gear you own. "Dad, are we really going fishing, just me and you, are we really?"

You groan and turn over, "Yes, son, but that's five days from now. You have plenty of time to get those things ready. Now go back to bed."

The next morning at 5:30 the same thing happens, but with one difference. This time as the little form comes into your darkened bedroom, the smell of dead fish hits your nose. You see, little boys don't know that minnows can't live in a bucket for five days! Every day the scene is repeated. Then on Friday evening the phone rings. It's a friend you haven't seen in years. He's going to be in town only one day—tomorrow. He wants you to play golf with him.

Early Saturday morning, your 6-year-old catches you creeping out of the house with your golf clubs. He is standing there with all the fishing equipment, ready to go.

"Daddy, what are you doing with your golf clubs? Aren't we going fishing like you said?"

You fall all over yourself, apologizing and making excuses.

"Just this time," you promise. "Next week we'll go fishing for sure."

But the next week something really big comes up—something over which you have no control. Your boss wants you to work on Saturday to get a major proposal ready. Surely your little boy will understand why you have to put off the fishing trip again.

You break the news to him and show him a brand new rod and reel you have bought for him.

"I promise, son. Next week we'll really, really go fishing!"

Your little boy throws the fishing rod down and runs back to his room, crying. "I don't ever want to go anywhere with you. I hate you!"

What happened? The person he loves and trusts the most has let him down. If you don't apologize and humble yourself, a cycle is set in motion: First, your child is hurt; hurt turns into lack of forgiveness, then into resentment; prolonged resentment becomes bitterness and finally, rebellion.

No child wakes up one morning deciding to become a rebel. Many times it springs from longstanding, unresolved hurt.

Recognizing Hurt and Bitterness

If you would like to know how to recognize hurt and bitterness, Bill Gothard suggest looking for these 10 signs in your child:

1. Shows a lack of concern for others. A bitter person cares very little about anybody else.

2. Is sensitive and touchy. For instance, if a bitter person walks into a room where two other people are talking, and those people get quieter as he walks in, the bitter person thinks, "They're talking about me."

3. Becomes very possessive with just a few friends, and rarely ever has any really close friends. Has an unnatural fear of losing his friends.

4. Tends to avoid meeting new people.

5. Shows little thankfulness or gratitude.

6. Usually will speak words of empty flattery or harsh criticism.

7. Holds grudges against people, often for a long, long time. He finds it extremely difficult to forgive.

8. Often has a stubborn or sulking attitude.

9. Is usually unwilling to share or help anybody.

10. Ends up experiencing mood extremes—very high and happy one minute, and the next thing you know, he's so low he can't reach up and touch bottom. [38]

Unfortunately, bitterness is a downward spiral; unless there is repentance and a choice to forgive those who have hurt him, the bitter person gets worse and worse. He begins to show the outward signs of withdrawal. Communication breaks down. He descends into stubborn sulkiness, and is openly rebellious and seeks out other rebels. The bitter one defends the wrong actions of the bad crowd he hangs out with, but quickly points his finger to condemn others.

For many, the end of the bitterness spiral is suicide. By killing himself, the bitter one is saying, "I'll punish the world by taking myself out of it. I'll teach them."

Some people think it is a sign of spirituality or strength if you don't have to humble yourself and ask your child to forgive you. Nothing could be further from the truth. It takes a big person to humble himself.

I heard Dr. James Dobson on the radio recently and he told a story about his family taking a ski trip. They were only to be there one week, but it snowed hard every day for six days, forcing them to stay inside their cabin. Finally, on the last day—a Sunday—it stopped snowing.

His teenaged daughter begged him, "Please, Dad, I know you don't let us do things like skiing on Sunday, but can't we skip church and do it? Just this once? Please? Oh, please?"

He stood there looking at his daughter's face and then glanced outside at the sunshine bouncing off the crusty snow. It would be a perfect day on the slopes—one good day to rescue an otherwise drab week. They would only be able to visit some strange church where they didn't know anyone and no one knew them, anyway. And surely they could worship the Lord while enjoying His beautiful creation?

"Okay, everybody. I know how much you've been looking forward to this trip. I guess it's okay if we miss church, just this once," he announced. Everyone quickly ran to pull on their ski clothes. Everyone except one—his 11-year-old son lagged behind.

Then Dr. Dobson noticed there were tears in his son's eyes. "Why son, what's the matter?" For a moment or two the boy didn't say anything, then he finally blurted, "Oh, Dad! It's just—I've never seen you back down on your convictions before!"

Dr. Dobson's heart smote him; he knew his son was right. What did it matter if he were the author of several best-selling Christian books on child rearing, the man who many thousands of people listened to weekly to hear his advice on how to have a Christian family? He had to be willing to receive correction from the Lord through his 11-year-old son. He quickly called the others back in, humbled himself before them and asked each of his children to forgive him for compromising his conviction.

That is spiritual greatness. And think of the strength of convictions his son is growing up with! Never be afraid to tell your kids you were wrong and to ask their forgiveness. There is no more powerful way to teach them right principles.

9

SAYING NO
WITHOUT A REASON

W<small>HEN</small> a child is between the ages of 12 to 13, something happens. First, he doesn't merely become thirteen; he becomes thirTEEN. All kinds of things start changing. For one thing, a "migrating spirit" comes upon him! Just like a wild bird following his instincts to head south for the winter, a 13-year-old cannot stay home on Friday and Saturday nights. Why? Because he is thirTEEN!

Do you want to know where every single teenager in the world goes on Friday and Saturday nights? They go SOME-WHERE. And who do they go with? EVERYBODY.

"But Mom, *everybody* is going *somewhere* Friday night!", they will say.

Let me give you a little look into the life of a typical teenager and her Mom and Dad. It's Friday and for some reason, 14-year-old Sally has come straight home. She didn't go out for a Coke, and she didn't stop at her best friend's house to look out the window and admire the good-looking boys passing by. No, she is home early for some strange reason. And she's acting very peculiar.

Sally walks into the kitchen and asks sweetly, "Mom, is there anything you want me to do? Shall I help clean up around the house?"

Mom stares at her in disbelief and considers taking her temperature and calling 911.

Instead she asks, "Well honey, have you cleaned up your room?"

"Oh yes, Mom. I've already done that."

Mother goes to check and again feels something very strange is going on. It is actually clean!

After more hard work, all the jobs are done. Sally checks the clock. Five-fifteen! In a few minutes, Dad will be home. She had better hurry and ask Mom before he gets here!

"Ummm...Mom. Everybody is going...umm...."

"...somewhere?" Mom ventures.

"Oh Mom! You mean you know about it? You knew what I was after all along? May I go Mom, please?"

Then Mom speaks those three dreaded words that every teenager hates to hear: "Ask your father."

So Sally switches quickly to Plan B.

Plan B is to comb her hair, wipe as much of her makeup off as she can and then sit demurely on the front steps to wait for her father.

Five-thirty, and Dad pulls unsuspectingly into the driveway. He barely gets out of the car when Sally runs and throws her arms around him and gives him a big kiss!

"Uh oh," he thinks. "She is definitely after something!"

But there's more. She follows him into the house with comments like, "Boy, Dad, is that a new suit?"

That throws him off guard.

"You know I told your mother if I held onto this suit long enough it would come back into style!" he replies.

Then she really hits below the belt. "Dad, I believe you are losing weight. Have you been dieting? You really look good, Dad, I mean it."

Dad is enjoying it now, and all his previous misgivings

65

have been swept away. Every father loves to hear things like this about himself even if he knows they really aren't true.

"You know, I was telling your mother that very thing just yesterday! I think I may have dropped a couple of pounds."

Then she brings out the big guns with, "Say, Dad, I think some of your hair is actually growing back in!! That 'Generation X' is really paying off!"

Dad's hand reaches tentatively to his thinning pate. Poor man. He's really falling for it now. He's thinking, "Wow, I'm such a good father. Those years of hard work and discipline and telling her those Bible stories—it's finally beginning to show!"

They're approaching the door now, and Sally realizes that she has to ask him The Question before they have to confront Mom. Otherwise, Mom will see Dad, give him "The Look," and he will know something is happening!

Hurriedly she pops the question: "Ummm, Dad—everybody is going somewhere tonight.... and uh, I was just wondering if..."

Suddenly the pieces come together in Dad's head. Teenager—suit—lost weight—hair...Somewhere! Everybody!" He's been led quite literally up the garden path!

Before his daughter gets to say another word he splutters, "No, no! no! no! no! Why can't you stay home on Friday nights? When I was your age, I didn't have to go running around every Friday and Saturday night, cruising in cars going round and round and round...! Why can't you just stay home like I did when I was your age?"

At this point Sally says, "Dad, when you were my age they didn't have cars!" One look and she changes her tone, fast. "Please, Dad?"

By this time, they're inside and Mom gives him "The Look." He starts yelling again, "No, no, no, no, no! I mean it—no!"

All is lost. Sally runs upstairs and calls her youth pastor on the phone. "Pastor John, (sniff) I can't come to the youth outing tonight (sob). My Dad and I are having communications problems (snuffle). Please pray for his wicked soul!"

When you were a kid, did your parents ever tell you "no" before you had a chance to ask them the whole question? Did they say "no" 16 times, and then add, "And I mean it?" Do you remember how much you hated that? Then why in the world do you do it to your children?

Perhaps you do it to your kids because you resented it when you were their age. You thought, "One of these days I'll grow up and I'll get to tell my kids 'no.'" Some parents really get into this. They enjoy saying "no" for no particular reason but to say "no."

What's wrong with this? It's wrong because it's against the pattern God gave us when He gave us rules. God never told us "no" because He enjoyed doing it. Deut. 6:24 says *all of His rules were given for our good and for our survival.*

I am not suggesting that you have to give your teenager a reason every time. But if he really needs to know, you better be able to give an answer. Occasionally that answer may be, "I can't explain it, honey, but I just don't feel right about you going there."

Don't ever say "no" without a reason. If you do, you are communicating that they are stupid.

Don't give your answer to a child's request until you have given him a chance to state his case. Otherwise, you are communicating that what your child has to say is unimportant.

Some parents say they don't listen because they know what their child is going to say anyway. No, you don't know. Even if you do, is it so much trouble to listen for 30 seconds? Hear what he has to say, then say "no" if you must. *But be sure to listen first.*

My wife has just about broken me of a bad habit. Often after speaking at a meeting, someone would come up to talk to me and my mind would be a million miles away. As the person started pouring out family problems, I'd be thinking about someone else I needed to talk to or something I had to hurry away for.

"Jacob!" Michelle said after one such experience, "How dare you look away while someone is talking to you like that! You are the most selfish, prideful person I have ever seen. That lady came to you about the real pain she's going through with her kids and you didn't even look her in the eye! If you're going to be in the ministry, you better start thinking of people as more important."

The truth hurt, but she was right. Now when people talk to me after a meeting I look right into their eyes. Even if I don't know the answers to give them, I can feel for them and give them my attention.

Jesus always cares about what people feel and listens to what they say to Him. If we as parents say "no" without listening, we can make our kids think we don't care what they think or feel. This provokes them to anger—just what the Word of God warns us not to do: "And now a word to you parents. Don't keep on scolding and nagging your children, making them angry and resentful. Rather, bring them up with the loving discipline the Lord himself approves, with suggestions and godly advice" (Ephs. 6:4, *The Living Bible*).

Another result of telling your child "no" without giving a reason is that it gives him less reason to trust you in the future. It also deprives him of learning from your past experience. You may have made the same mistake you're warning him away from—perhaps you need to share with him what happened to you.

Moreover, withholding the reason for a "no" enforces what the devil is telling your child already: "Your parents don't understand. They're so unfair! They just don't want you to have any fun." Charles Stanley once said, "By listening to your kids today, you earn the right to be heard tomorrow." If you refuse to hear them, they will stop coming to you.

There may be occasions when you have to say "no" and your teenager can't understand why. But if this is an exception and your son or daughter knows that you only say "no" when you have a reason, they will believe that you are saying it because you love them.

Perhaps you are fearful your children may make a choice that could hurt them. There are some mistakes you can't allow them to make, but they need to be able to make some choices on their own.

Did you make any wrong choices when you were young? Have you made any wrong choices lately? How do you expect your children not to make any? If you invest enough of God's Word into their lives, and quality time when it's time for them to make choices, they'll make right ones.

TIPS FOR PARENTS

•As a parent you should realize that apologizing in humility is a sign of strength, and not weakness.

•When apologizing to your children, include your need for God's forgiveness as your authority for the basis of your action.

•If you notice that your child has been hurt or disappointed, set aside private time for the matter to be discussed and do not be satisfied until it has been resolved.

•Become an effective listener. Give your children your full attention when they want to talk. This strengthens their self-esteem.

•Take time to listen to all of the details of a proposal from your child before making a ruling. Have objective reasons to support your answer.

10

POWER PLAYS

W HEN parents don't relate to their children and simply lay down rules for them to obey, it can cause them to rebel. The Bible always ties rules to good relationships—you cannot have one without the other. Jesus linked loving Him with keeping His commandments (John 15:14).

In the Old Testament, when the children of Israel and Moses were at Mount Sinai, the people begged him to go meet with God and get the commandments for them. Moses had a relationship with God, but they avoided knowing God for themselves. He brought back the commandments of God to them, but they didn't keep them. Only Moses—the one who knew God—kept His commandments. The Children of Israel didn't have a relationship with God, and rebellion followed.

Probably the greatest source of pain in families is the absence of a loving relationship between family members. Relationships require setting priorities; there are no short-cuts to relationships—they take time. Never forget that children spell love "T.I.M.E." I have already mentioned how the average parent spends not more than two minutes a day communicating with his children. (Time spent giving orders or correction isn't counted.) That's only two minutes of real communication, where the parent not only speaks but listens. Some experts believe this is a contributing factor to the rise of homosexuality and premarital sex, as well as other social problems increasing among young people. In a recent survey 8,000 teenagers were asked, "If there were only one person you could spend time with, who would you want it to be? Not one out of the 8,000 named an adult. Perhaps we are being cast aside by a generation that we have ignored.

In a day when we have "instant this" and "instant that," we are discovering there is no other way to give our children quality time other than giving them quality time. Microwave chicken might taste just fine, but our relationships with our children can't be reduced to seconds a day. Otherwise, we'll find our children ending up like some microwave casseroles—fine on the outside but hard and cold on the inside!

Perhaps this is why young people described by their teachers and friends as totally normal end up being written about in the newspaper after committing some vile crime. On the outside, they appear well-dressed, well-fed, and well-educated, but internally it's a different story.

Take Ann, for instance. Ann was 13, an only child, and an honors student in a private school in Maryland. She seemed to be a model student and a devoted daughter. But one night Ann brought two neighborhood boys into her bedroom and called for her father to come upstairs. The three teenagers used a knife and a piece of pipe to stab and bludgeon Ann's father to death. [39]

Stories like Ann's aren't that uncommon, either. Every year in the United States, 300 teenagers kill either their mother or father. According to the National Institute of Mental Health, one in 20 families with adolescent children have teens who are abusing their parents. Listen to some of their comments in a group therapy session:

> Soon the shoves turned to pokes, then hard jabs, sometimes punches. Sure, I tried to fight back until

one day she beat me up, smashing my head into the floor—completely overpowered me....

A large, stocky man in his forties says,
I have three boys...the other day my youngest, 13, held me in a stranglehold so tight I couldn't get out. I was so shocked....

A mother of a 16-year-old shares,
Our daughter had me terrorized. Joyce was so destructive that there isn't a room in our house which doesn't bear testimony to her abuse. Once she came flying at me with a kitchen knife...at one time we were so desperate my husband and I actually paid her not to hit me.[40]

Other angry young people just run away from home. In fact nearly one million leave home each year. Many end up on the streets of Los Angeles, New York or other cities as girl or boy prostitutes.

For some, their rage turns inward, and they join the thousands of teens who kill themselves every year.

When interviewing teens who had tried to kill themselves, the National Institute for Mental Health found that 93 percent reported a lack of communication between them and their parents. [41]

No communication. No relationship. Only rules. Little wonder that we reap a tragic harvest in our young people.

Ann, the girl who stabbed her father to death, could represent so many homes where there are rules without relationships.

In Ann's case, her father chose all of her clothes and her friends. He refused to let her leave the house except to go to school; the few exceptions were when she was allowed to have friends over, but even then he kept a watchful eye on them. When Ann began to rebel, he yanked her out of her school and enrolled her in a stricter one. And when he couldn't stop her from seeing some boys in the neighborhood, he put his house up for sale and told the family they were moving. That was when Ann struck back.

Experts point to fury like this and say one reason for such abnormal stress in teenagers is the prevalence of divorce and working mothers. Parents just can't spend the time with children they used to, and young people facing other problems are left without their parents' attention at a time in their life when they need it most. [42]

The Bible speaks in Exodus 20:5 of the sins of the fathers being visited on the children to the third and fourth generations. Divorce is a sin which clearly demonstrates this biblical principle.

Divorce is the result of broken relationships, and often it is the fruit of earlier broken relationships. If you are divorced, it is possible that you also came from a broken home and that the seeds of your divorce came from your parents' divorce.

Why is this true? The parent with whom you were raised had to bear a double burden and it was probably impossible for her to spend much time with you. Also, you had no role models showing you how a husband and a wife work out their problems in everyday life. Through no fault of your own, you failed to learn how to treat a man or a woman well because you weren't able to grow up watching a stable marital relationship, with people responding to conflicts in a godly way. Much of what we do as adults is based on unconscious modeling in our early childhood.

If you are saying, "Yes, that's my story," I want to tell you: Please, don't despair! I know what you have gone through. I came from a troubled home and yet God was able to re-create my responses and show me how to overcome my past when I married Michelle. If God can do it for me, He can do it for you, too.

It is particularly difficult to have a good relationship with your child if there has been a divorce in your home. Unless you break the cycle with the help of the Holy Spirit, your kids will pass on the effects of a broken relationship to their children. Real problems you have faced in your life will be repeated in your children's lives. That is what the Bible means by the sins of the fathers being visited on children to the third and fourth generations.

You must have a good relationship with your children in order to effectively discipline them. Don't you find that you can receive correction more easily from a friend who really loves you than from a stranger? When your son or daughter knows you love them, they will allow you to speak into their lives in a special way. One psychologist says: for every one time you correct a child, you need to approve them twenty times to keep your relationship in balance.

Divorce isn't the only thing hurting homes today. If both parents are working, there is a real probability that relationships in the home are suffering. Parents who are gone all the time are little better than no parents at all.

In some cases, it is absolutely necessary for both parents to work. Perhaps you are in such a situation—you're not working to enjoy added luxuries, but simply to pay the rent, utilities, and food bill. If that is true, then you will need to work extra hard to find creative ways to compensate for your absence.

It is not God's first choice to have both parents away all day working. He intended the family to have a center—one person who would be there to nurture and train children as her primary responsibility.

Often, women are going back to work because they are not valued as homemakers. Their husbands belittle their roles and society portrays them as old-fashioned, afraid to face the "real world" and compete and prove themselves.

Remember the way your mother introduced herself? "Oh, I'm just a housewife."

Women became convinced they could not be fulfilled unless they were working outside the home. Now we are reaping the results of this tragedy in a massive way.

Besides time spent together, another thing is needed in the home. Openness and a willingness to be vulnerable are needed for good relationships. Perhaps you came from a family that didn't verbalize its feelings; as a result, you now have a hard time saying "I love you."

This is another bondage which you will pass on to your children if you don't break it now. Ask God to help you open up and be transparent with your wife or husband and with your children and expose your feelings.

It may sound funny, but when Adam and Eve were in their perfect state they were naked. I'm certainly not advocating nudism, but there is a truth to be learned here: Ever since sin came into the world, we've been trying to cover up. We not only want to cover our bodies—we want to cover up everything. We fear being seen for who we really are. Parents fear their children seeing their true feelings; they may fear that their children will not love them if they really know them.

The Josh McDowell Ministry recently polled 50 young women at a large church. They were each asked, "Do you have a relationship with your Dad where you really communicate with him? Do you have that with your Mom?" Twenty-five said they had that kind of relationship with their mother, but almost no one had that with their father.

God has given us the responsibility to nurture the relationships He has given us. It isn't your child's job to make sure he has open communication with you; it's your job. Make the effort to open up to your kids. Listen to them. It doesn't matter if you are not "into" skateboarding or video games or the latest clothing fads. What counts is that you are interested in them. That means you try to be interested in anything that is important to them. Keep in mind: rules without relationships lead to rebellion every time.

TIPS FOR PARENTS

•Determine that developing quality time with your children is going to be a priority.

•Set aside specific times to spend with each child. This includes fathers as well as mothers.

•Have times when the children choose the activity or the place you are going.

•Make it a point to verbally and physically express your love to your children each day.

•Point out the positive characteristics of your children with praise, rather than emphasizing the negative.

11
WHEN PARENTS
USE POWER
INSTEAD OF AUTHORITY

"SON," Dad barks, "Take out that trash." "But Dad..."
"Boy, don't you 'but Dad' me! I'll knock you out! Don't you tell
me, 'But Dad'! I'll throw you right through that wall!"

Using sheer physical force may control your child when he
is little, but what happens when he's six inches taller than
you? That's when you better have authority with your son,
not just power.

There is a big difference between power and authority, yet
many confuse the two. Let me give you an example.

My wife weighs about 105 pounds, and she is 5 feet, 6
inches tall; I am six-foot, three inches tall and weigh 190.

If I say to Michelle, "Honey, would you get me a cup of
coffee?" what do you think happens? If she responds, "Well,
baby, why don't you get your own coffee?" do I grab her and
yell, "Woman, how would you like six weeks in intensive
care?"

I could do that. I outweigh her. I'm bigger than she is. I

have the power to do it.

Yet, I don't have to threaten her. She does what I ask her to do most of the time......(well, some of the time......alright, occasionally!) because she finds security in me. What I have with my wife is not power but authority.

You might be stronger than your child, but that doesn't give you the authority to do whatever you want to do. For instance, you don't have the authority to beat on your kids instead of disciplining them properly.

Here's another illustration of the difference between power and authority: You pull up to a red light driving a car that was tested on the Nevada Salt Flats at 130 miles an hour. Can you run that red light if you want to and roar through town at the speed in which your car will go? You have the power to do it, but in case you're not sure if you have the authority, try doing it and find out! Your local highway patrolman is an expert teacher of the difference between power and authority.

Authority is something we are given by God. "Everyone must submit himself to the governing authorities," says Paul in Romans, "For there is no authority except that which God has established. The authorities that exist have been established by God. Consequently, he who rebels against the authority is rebelling against what God has instituted, and those who do so will bring judgment on themselves." (Romans 13:1,2 NIV)

As parents, we are in the home as God's authority over our children; but we ourselves are also under His authority. We must answer to Him concerning the way we carry out the responsibilities with which He has entrusted us.

When someone exercises loving, God-given authority, people respond. Have you ever seen a little-bitty grandma who weighs all of 90 pounds telling some big, hulking grandson what to do? He does it meekly and immediately. She isn't exercising power. She has authority.

The danger of using power instead of authority is that it

provokes rebellion. One power play provokes another in response.

In a marriage, a husband may threaten, "Dear, if you don't do such-and-such, I'll take your checkbook away!"

The wife answers, "Oh yeah? Well, why don't you sleep with that checkbook on the couch tonight!"

Neither your relationship with your spouse nor your relationship with your children should be a battle of power. If you respond in a firm, loving, godly manner as you carry out authority in the home, there will be far less likelihood of your kids turning on you someday in rebellion.

God gave us the first years of our children's lives to earn their trust as authority figures. While they are small and dependent, we are to exercise power justly through needed spankings. Gradually, as they grow in strength, they also learn to respect our authority, not just the physical force we have over them. In God's wisdom, their respect for us grows even as our strength diminishes and theirs increases.

TIPS FOR PARENTS

•Children respect parents who use authority with responsibility. Using power as a substitute for authority only alienates children and lessens their respect for you.

•Make a list of the characteristics of the relationship between God and His children. Use this list as a pattern for your relationship with your children.

•Keep your relationship with God open and clear. He is your authority and is a foundation for you as a parent who is the proper authority to your children.

12
TOO MUCH, TOO SOON, TOO FAST

A common pitfall for parents is to try and live their lives through their kids. They want their children to be all that they were or weren't—they have to be the best at everything. Their children are pushed to achieve, beginning with pre-school. Some preschools offer highly academic programs, and there are even crib toys designed to help babies be ready to learn to read sooner.

Even outside of school, parents' ambitions can drive their children.

One boy in my home town is on three different athletic teams, a schedule he maintains in addition to his school work. His father can be seen, urging his 10-year-old on from the sidelines, furious if the boy messes up a play.

For the girls, there may be a progression of ballet classes, gymnastics, music—all good things, but sometimes leaving so little time for them to be little girls. There are even beauty pageants, starting from baby contests and going straight through every age level until the girls are old enough to compete for Miss America. Gone are the days of pigtails and simple starched dresses. They now have Lee press-on nails—artificial finger nails for little girls, and fifth graders go to school wearing makeup. Fashions for boys and girls feature the miniature adult look. In so many ways the pressure is on for children to grow up overnight.

I watched a television interview of a young girl and her mother; the girl was a skater competing in the Winter Olympics. Her mother evidently accompanied her to competitions and made sure she kept up her vigorous training schedule.

The young skater said, "I went through a time when it was really hard and I wanted to quit." (She had received a silver medal earlier, but then she was injured in a fall.)

"I've been trying to come back," she told the interviewer.

"No," her mom interrupted, on camera, "You haven't been trying to come back. You haven't really been working at it. If you really wanted this, you could have it!"

I stared at the television in amazement. The woman must be trying to live her life through this poor girl, I thought. And what irony for a young teen to be struggling to make a comeback.

Pressures from outside the family are also robbing children of their childhood.

Dr. Peter Stursberger of the American Academy of Pediatrics says these are the most dangerous times adolescents have ever had to face—short of actual war.[43] They must make choices at younger ages and with less parental input than ever before.

Fourteen-and 15-year-olds have to decide, "Am I going to have sex? Am I going to smoke pot? Am I going to drink beer?" Those choices used to be made in college; now they're being made by children in elementary and junior high school.

The breakdown of the family has increased the influence teenagers have on one another. Young people are forced to gravitate toward friends as a substitute for the understanding, acceptance, and direction not received at home. The crowd often pressures the teen into something he doesn't really want to do, but he does it rather than risk the disapproval of the group.

Just because other parents are doing it, you don't have to allow your little 10-year-old girl to dress like a college student or use makeup. Neither do you have to shove your boy into cut-throat athletic competition just because other parents act like an NFL draft choice is just around the corner for their son. Don't allow your children to be pushed too fast by others. Allow your kids to be kids.

Television is still another force that can rob children of their childhood. Television shows geared for the 30-year-old are also watched by the 11-year-old. Viewing adult programming helps to sweep away childhood innocence, breaking down barriers between children and the adult world. What were once considered to be adult themes are now shown to the entire family—violence, death, sex. Parents have to explain to their children sexual aberrations, occult symbols, and gruesome cruelties that they themselves probably never heard of until they were in their twenties.

Divorce also steals away childhood. Children see things like a boyfriend coming over to sleep with Mom invading what used to be a private, precious thing—the home. Also, with a single parent struggling to support the kids, older children must become little parents, helping to supervise the younger children and get dinner started. Many kids are losing out on what childhood is all about: innocence, joy, and play. They're taking on responsibilities that some people 30 years of age have trouble handling.

I grew up in a ghetto in Houston, Texas. Sometimes when I share my testimony, people marvel at the things I was involved in when I was nine, 10 or 11 years old: drugs, sexual immorality, robbery, and violence.

Someone said, "There are no children in the ghetto; only

small people." Now, our whole society has come to this. There aren't innocent children anymore—only small people.

We have assumed that because we live in the "Age of Information," we must instill knowledge in our children. Yet it is more important to instill values in children, rather than just give them information, and values are much more difficult and time-consuming to teach. There is information that your child isn't ready for. We must concentrate on instilling values in our children, and let them stay innocent of some things until it is an appropriate time for adult information to be taught.

Sins of the Fathers

If there is an area in your life as a parent which is not under the control of God, you can deal with it now or you can wait about 15 years and try to deal with it in your child's life.

The Bible says in Exodus 20:5 that the sins of the father affect the children. This doesn't mean that every child of an alcoholic becomes an alcoholic, but the chances are greater that he will. Everyone still has freedom of choice and can choose not to go the way of his parents in sin. But he has areas of weakness—both genetic and environmental predispositions—and blind spots which the enemy can more easily penetrate because of his parents' sins.

Some of the great men of the Bible had moral flaws which were exactly repeated in their children after them. Abraham deceived two kings, telling them his wife was his sister; Isaac committed the same sin; Jacob followed his grandfather and father's example but his deception took a different, more hurtful bent—he deceived his own blind, aged father, Isaac.

Another story illustrating repetition of moral flaws is that of David. He committed sexual sin, giving in to his lust with Bathsheba. He reaped that same sin with his son Amnon, who raped his half-sister, Tamar. David's son Solomon also had a great weakness for women, leading ultimately to his spiritual downfall.

A family I know illustrates the principle of fathers passing sins to the children. The great-grandfather was a womanizer who abandoned his wife, leaving her with many children. His son came to the United States from Mexico, but until his conversion a few years before his death, he repeated the immorality of his father.

That man's son had 12 children. Three-fourths of those children were divorced because of immorality. In the succeeding generation, it was the same except with increased numbers. It became a huge pyramid of immorality and divorce, multiplying with each succeeding generation.

Except for the grace of God and the blood of Jesus, such a chain can continue in a family for many years. Jesus does break the curse of generations, but without Him we are almost programmed to repeat our parents' sins. We need to ask God for discernment concerning family weaknesses and break those chains in prayer.

Kids Rebel Because They Have Free Will

In the past three chapters, we have seen many factors which can lead to the rebellion of a child. But there is still one more—a mystery factor. You can do everything right and yet a child can rebel because he has a free will.

I know of one home where two sons were raised in a godly environment with parents in the ministry. They invested themselves into those two boys, exposed them to biblical teaching all their lives, sent them to Christian schools, prayed for them and taught them and loved them both. Yet one son turned out like a saint and the other like a devil—promiscuous, on drugs, and breaking his parents' hearts. Why? Because of free will.

In situations like this, parents rack their brains and souls, trying to figure out what they did wrong. Then people come along and heap more condemnation on them.

Ninety percent of what kids are is a reflection of their home. But there's another factor that goes beyond influence and that is the freedom of the will. Before you blame yourself, remember: Jesus was the most loving authority to ever walk on this earth, and He had one of His 12 rebel against Him.

Adam and Eve had the perfect father—God Himself—and yet they rebelled.

One of the favorite parables of Jesus was that of the prodigal son. That son had a godly father who did everything right, yet the prodigal used his free will to rebel.

You can do everything right and still have your heart broken by a rebellious child. You also can have hope, as He does, for every prodigal to come home. But first we will see in the next chapter some warnings you can give to your rebel.

TIPS FOR PARENTS

• Analyze the schedule of your children and the family as a whole. Make a list of the priority activities your children desire most, not what you desire for them.

• As the parent, make sure that your child's life is filled with the activities of a child. Do not let them be over-run by a mindset and lifestyle that exceeds their age.

• Check the values of your home. Where do they originate?

• You need to instill your values in your children, not those of the media. A child who receives values from a secular worldly source will develop into a secular and worldly young person.

• Examine your own life. Do you see weakness that is also now in your children? If you do, go to your children and confess this area of weakness to them. Tell them that you don't want to see the same thing happen to them, or even to their children. Break the cycle now!

13

How To Warn A Rebel

IF your child is a rebel, you must warn him of several things:

Tell your child he is eventually going to have to accept someone's authority.

If it's not yours, then it will have to be someone else's—the boss on his job, the police, someone.

The rebel believes his parents are his problem; he needs to be told that he is rebelling not just against his parents but against all authority—teachers, law, every authority. He is living on immediate thrills and hasn't come to grips with this understanding. He doesn't see that Satan offers quick thrills with long-term suffering. What God provides is temporary hard work, or self-control, with long-term rewards.

Don't emphasize that your teenager is in rebellion against you personally. God is the One who put authorities, including parents, over us all. Tell your teenager that because he is refusing to accept those in direct authority over him—his parents—he is in rebellion against God, because all authority, including yours, comes from Him. (Romans 13:1)

Tell your child that rebellion has built-in judgment.

If someone jumps off a building and breaks his leg, is it the fault of the person who built the building? No, because the law of gravity states that if you jump from high places, you will fall, and it will hurt.

It is very important to tell your children this because God has set up laws concerning authority. The way we respond to those laws is just as important as how we respond to the laws of nature, such as gravity.

Warn your child that rebellion is deceptive.

When someone is in rebellion, he makes himself believe that everyone who loves him and is in authority over him is bad—beginning with God, Mom and Dad, teachers, even friends who tell him he is doing wrong. The rebel ends up running from God like He was the devil and to the devil like he was God. When a person thinks the ones who love him hate him, and the people that hate him are the ones who love him, that is deception.

The rebel needs to know that rebellion is witchcraft. (Sam. 15:23)

How is rebellion witchcraft? Because the first individual to rebel was the devil. Satan's sin was that he, the created one, thought he was equal with the Creator—that was his sin.

Satan said to himself, "I don't need to obey God, the authority over me. I'm smart enough, I can do everything on my own."

Think how insane that was: to be in the literal presence of God, to see Him and yet to think yourself equal to Him.

Satan thought, "I don't have to do what God wants me to do. I am wiser—I can be trusted more. I'm going to trust myself, not God."

It's the same with the human rebel. He says, "I, the created, don't have to listen to the Creator. I'm as smart as He is. I know what's better for me than He does!" A young person

87

may say, "I, the child, don't have to listen to my parents. I'm as smart as they are. I don't have to obey them."

When he does that, he puts himself in alliance with Satan and is saying the same thing the devil did when he was cast out of heaven.

Webster's Dictionary defines rebellion as, "Opposition to one in authority or control; open defiance of or resistance to an established government."

That is Satan's intention: To encourage children to overthrow their established government, their parents, and to usurp their authority and God's.

WARNING TO A REBEL

Prov. 29:1   He who being often reproved hardens his neck, shall suddenly be destroyed, and that without remedy. (A.V.)

Prov. 16:5   Every one proud and arrogant in heart is disguising, hateful and exceedingly offensive to the Lord: be assured—I pledge it he will not go unpunished. (A.V.)

WHEN REBELS DON'T LISTEN

Prov. 15:32 He who refuses and ignores instruction and correction despises himself, but he who heeds reproof gets understanding. (A.V.)

Prov. 15:5   A fool despises his father's instruction and correction, but he who regards reproof acquires prudence. (A.V.)

Prov. 15: 10 There is severe discipline for him who forsakes God's way, and he who hates reproof will die. [physically, morally, and spiritually] (A.V.)

Prov. 13:18 Poverty and shame shall be to him who refuses instruction and correction, but he who needs reproof shall be honored. (A.V.)

TIPS FOR PARENTS

• Ignoring a problem never solves it, it only prolongs it. Decide that a firm warning must be given.

• Go over the warning with your children and see what their reaction to truth is.

• If possible, state what the consequences to their rebellion could be. Try to get them to understand that they are personally responsible for what happens as a result of their behavior.

14

THE ROAD TO DECEPTION

IN the early part of this book, we talked about the war that is being waged on children today. There is another war being fought and it is a far older conflict. It came to this planet thousands of years ago in the Garden of Eden. It is a war on the reputation of God—a diabolically clever, unrelenting battle to destroy the perception people have of God's nature and character.

In Genesis 3, Satan fired his first volley at Eve to destroy her opinion of God.

In verse one, he approached Eve as a serpent and slid in a sly distortion: "Really?" he asked. None of the fruit in the garden? God says you mustn't eat any of it?" (Gen. 3:1, *The Living Bible*)

He didn't start off with a blatant lie. He took what God said and exaggerated it, implying that God wanted to keep everything good from Adam and Eve.

Eve explained to the serpent what God actually said; that they were able to eat from all of the fruit trees in the Garden except one, and that if they ate from that tree, they would die.

Then the serpent grew more bold. "That's a lie! he hissed. "You'll not die!"

The serpent then took the next step in his deception—he mixed in some truth with the lie.

Satan mixed in some facts with his poison; he said, "God knows that in the day you eat of it your eyes will be opened, and you will be *like God*, knowing good and evil." (Gen. 3:5 NKJ, emphasis mine).

It was true that Adam and Eve would know good and evil—they would lose their innocence forever. But they would not be like God. Instead, they would become their own gods.

From the Garden of Eden until now, Satan has never changed his basic strategy. His intention is still to give man a distorted view of who God is. He still whispers his Number One Lie to us: "God is selfish. He wants to rip you off. If you live for God, you're going to miss everything." Most people believe him.

How incredible it is that most people think a good, loving God, whose only desire is to share His great life with them, is actually selfish and determined to take things away from them.

Something happened to me several years ago that illustrates how foolish this is.

One evening I was getting ready to leave our house to go to a speaking engagement when someone ran up and began to pound on our front door. I opened it to see a thin man holding his head with one hand. A trickle of blood was running down his unshaven face.

He screamed, "Let me in, man! Please, let me in! They're after me! Please, please, don't let them catch me!"

I let him in and we ran to the window to look out. Sure enough, there were two angry men standing outside on the street. One was wielding a wooden fence post like a baseball bat. My unexpected visitor quickly told me these men were chasing him to settle a score from a previous fight. He showed me that he had been hit in the head by the fence post. He continued to beg, "Please, don't let those men get me! Please save me!"

We called the police and waited for them to come. This experience made me think: what if I had opened my door to a man being pursued and he told me that someone was running after him, trying to give him eternal life? The person chasing him wanted him to be happy, to bless him for the rest of his life and throughout eternity, and he just had to get away before he was caught! Ridiculous? Yet this is exactly what rebels are doing—running from the One who loves them the most.

Satan's attack on God's reputation has continued throughout the centuries, and whether you know it or not, you have been subjected to it. Even Christians have a distorted view of God. Why else would we hold back from giving our all to Him?

Have you ever been convinced that if you stepped out of line just once and did something wrong, God would be waiting to zap you with some horrible punishment? Perhaps your parents used the threat of God's disapproval as a scare tactic to keep you in line, like the line from the country and western song, "God's gonna git ya fer that!"

How many people believe that if they get sick it's because they did something wrong and God is punishing them? They examine their hearts, searching for some tiny, secret sin that allowed the horrible thing to happen to them.

What does that say about God's character? I wouldn't do something like that to my little boy, and I'm not nearly as good as God is. Do I watch outside the door, waiting for Daddy Boy to do something wrong so I can spank him for the slightest infraction?

Or what if something goes wrong with your business? Do you decide you have missed that "elusive" will of God again? (After all, everyone knows how very *hard* God makes it to find out what He wants you to do.)

Our distorted view of God also makes it difficult to trust Him. We don't believe deep down that God wants to heal us. So we listen to all the faith preachers we can, urging us to read and re-read all the verses in the Bible where God promises healing. Our faith must be rooted in who God is. The One who made all the promises is the One to have faith in, not just the words themselves. *He does good things because of who He is.* Our faith should be in Him, not just in a list of Bible references.

As we come to know God and His true character, Satan's attempts to smear Him won't work. We judge what we hear on the basis of what we know about a person. You aren't as likely to believe a wild rumor about a personal friend as you are about someone you hardly know. It should be the same with our knowledge of God. Firm belief in the true character of God will thwart Satan's attempts to undermine our view of Him.

The road to deception begins with a distorted view of God.

Jesus told a story in Matthew 25 that illustrates this deception. Jesus told of a man about to go on a long trip who entrusted some of his money to three slaves to invest for him. To one, he gave 5,000 talents or dollars; to the second 2,000, and to the last, 1,000, according to their abilities. Then he left.

You remember the story. The man with 5,000 immediately began to invest it and soon doubled the amount. The second slave also doubled his master's money. But the slave who received 1,000 dug a hole in the ground and buried it.

Even though this is a very familiar parable of Jesus, you should look closely for one thing: look at the character of the master and then see how the third slave perceived his character. Here was a man who entrusted money to his slaves to invest for him, then turned around and gave it to them to use for themselves, rewarding the two men generously and promoting them. He was a trusting, encouraging, loving, faithful master. He owned these slaves; they were his property. He owned the money he had given them to invest. Yet he treated them as partners in the end.

Now listen to the words of the servant who buried the money: "Sir, I knew you were a hard man, and I was afraid

93

you would rob me of what I earned, so I hid your money in the earth and here it is!" (Matt. 25:24,25, *The Living Bible*)

Was the third slave talking about the same man? First we saw the actions of a trusting, encouraging, loving, faithful man, and then heard him described as a hard man, as a thief, and someone to fear. This same master had just given away the returns from his own large investment to his slaves. It is clear that the third slave had a distorted view of his master, and that this distortion deceived. So it is with a person who has a distorted view of God.

There's something else to note about this story. The first two slaves understood that they belonged to their master and the money they were using was his, too. He had gone down to the slave market and outbid other potential owners to bring those three men back as his property.

To whom do we belong? If we do what we want with our lives instead of obeying Him, we are stealing from Him. That is what's wrong with a rebel: The rebel has stolen his life from its rightful owner. Because of that, he has a distorted idea about God. He believes God—who is trusting, loving, faithful, and fair—is hard, vengeful, and someone to be feared.

Once started on the road to deception, the good becomes bad and the bad becomes good. The distortion starts with a person's view of God, but then it progresses to create other problems.

Look at the teenage rebel. Next to God, who loves him the most in the world? His parents. But once on the road to deception, Mom and Dad soon become the "old man" and the "old lady."

He fumes, "My old man and my old lady are my biggest problems! One of these days I'm gonna get out of this house. I'm gonna get me a fast car and a stereo and I'm gonna plug in Van Halen with my 5-million-watt booster, and I'm gonna shake houses three blocks away! Nobody's gonna tell me when to come in and who to go out with, when to clean my room.... I'm gonna do anything I wanna do, when I wanna do it, and how I wanna do it. I'll have it made!"

The distortion continues. All other authority figures become the enemy. The police become the "pigs." He becomes convinced that his teachers live their lives planning torment just for him. His English teacher hates him and only him. The first day he walked into class, she must have looked at him and said, "There are three things I don't like about you: The first is your face, and the other two are anything else that's a part of you. I don't like you." She might not have said it, but he feels that she must have thought it.

The next person to become bad in the eyes of the rebel is any spiritual leader—the youth pastor, a Sunday School teacher, or anyone who tries to tell him what to do. You see, all authority flows from God, and once the rebel turns away from God, all other authority figures become his enemies.

Even friends become the enemy, if they are the kind that remind the rebel that what he is doing is wrong. He gets new friends—those old ones didn't really care about him. The rebel ends up running from everyone who really cares about him.

The deception ends in how the rebel views himself. Because we are made in the image of God, if we get a distorted view of Him, we can't see the truth about ourselves.

Why else would rebels do what they do, abusing themselves, thinking they're having a good time? Because they have a distorted view.

There are two basic distortions as the rebel views himself: One way is to see himself like a god—the center of attention, someone who can do no wrong. All his problems come from other people. The second distortion is that he thinks he is worthless—he can't do anything right and he never will.

There's only one answer for both of these distortions. Only the Gospel can restore a right idea of what God is like and a right idea of who we are.

15
Hope For
The Homecoming

Perhaps you have read up to this point with a growing sense of despair. As we have looked at the Word of God and showed many of the patterns of teenage rebellion, you may have felt like giving up.

Perhaps your heart is crying out, "I've done everything wrong! There's no hope! My (daughter or son) has gone too far. The hurts have been too deep, there's no hope."

Or, you may have checked out the table of contents and were so desperate over your child's condition that you have come straight to this chapter. In either case, it is important to keep what we have been learning about the character of God firmly in your mind. He is not a God who holds what we have done wrong against us. He is, always, the God of the second chance, or as I often tell young people, "God's not mad at you. As long as there is breath in our bodies, He is there, waiting to help us and give us hope." There is hope for the homecoming of your rebel child. God the Father knows intimately the pain you're going through. You see, He has felt it many times Himself.

Jesus made that clear when He told that most famous of all the parables: the story of a rebel son. Not only do we see in this parable the way God shares our broken hearts over wayward children, but we learn several steps to follow to help a prodigal come home.

Actually, it was the story of two rebel sons: The older one was a compliant rebel. He came in when he was supposed to, and he didn't go where his parents didn't want him to—but in his heart he had quietly rebelled and become bitter toward his parents.

The other son, the younger one, became known as the prodigal. He was openly defiant of his father's will and what was expected of him.

He told his father, "I want my share of your estate now, instead of waiting until you die!"

He was sick and tired of hanging around that place. He wanted something more glamorous than farming. He wanted to party in the big city. And he knew if he was going to do what he wanted, he'd have to get away from his father and his rules. He couldn't openly rebel and stay there.

This is our first lesson in hope for a homecoming. *You cannot allow your son or daughter to stay under your roof if he or she will not live by your rules.*

The prodigal son knew he couldn't get away with doing all he wanted to do if he stayed at home. He had to get away. Far away. He didn't come from one of those homes where kids are allowed to do anything—drink, do drugs, sleep around—with their parents afraid to confront them. If he was going to live wild, he knew he had to leave.

When a child openly defies your authority in the home, it is time for him to leave. This doesn't mean he has to love God to stay there. But if your rules are to be in at 11:00, he must be in at 11:00. He may not be a Christian, but if your rules are to go to church on Sunday, he must go.

A close friend of mine related how he once had been forced to tell his son to leave home. The teenage boy had openly defied authority and lied repeatedly to his parents.

My friend said it was one of the toughest decisions he had ever made and often questioned whether it was the right choice.

However, a few months later the boy came to visit my friend in his office. They talked about several things — how his Mom was doing, about his sister, home.

Then the boy looked straight into his Dad's eyes, and with tears falling off his cheeks, said, "Dad, little by little I'm beginning to understand what you and Mom were trying to teach me all those years."

Today that boy has turned his life around and is a genuine witness for the Lord, active in church, happily married to a fine Christian girl — and forever grateful to his Mom and Dad who refused to compromise truth and right.

Parents are so timid when it comes to enforcing spiritual rules. No one fears that children who are forced to eat their vegetables will grow up to be adults who hate vegetables. Yet, so many are afraid to make their kids go to church.

"They may learn to hate church, so I can't force them, some say." Why is that reasoning only applied to spiritual things?

I know of a young lady who went through a period of rebellion against her godly parents for a number of years. Yet throughout the ordeal, her parents made her kneel whenever the family had their devotions. She even had to pray, and bow her knee to God. A few years later, she fully repented. Today she is my wife.

If your child becomes openly defiant of you and of God's authority, which you represent—if the child won't obey your rules and won't at least do the outward things, like going to church—it's time for that child to go.

This may seem impossible. You may feel that there's more hope for change if your child is still under your roof, but that may not be so. If a child has openly moved away in her heart, you are allowing that child to trample upon your principles and casting aside any hope of gaining your child's respect and spiritual return.

The story of the prodigal son goes on to say that the father agreed to divide his wealth between his sons. He gave him his inheritance and he let him go. This was a real step of faith on the father's part.

Many of us would have said, "If you think you're getting your inheritance now, you have another thing coming!"

But the father allowed him to make some choices on his own. He knew where his son was headed and what he intended to do with that money, but he didn't beg him to stay. He let him do it.

The young man had his joy ride and his cheap thrills. He went to a distant land and wasted all his money on parties and prostitutes.

Then, when his money was all gone, a famine hit and the prodigal began to starve. All of his new friends deserted him, and no one helped him. The only work he could get was working in a pig pen, a lowly, degrading job.

This is our next lesson for the homecoming: *Parents of prodigals need to allow their kids to reach their own "pig pens" to find out what hitting bottom is really like.*

Instead, I have more than once seen parents pray, "Oh, God, bring him to his senses. Do whatever you have to do to get his attention and change him!"

Then when God begins working in the situation, pulling away all the props around that wayward child, suddenly the parents dive in to rescue the child from his pig pen before he ever reaches it; sinking into slop themselves up to their necks, holding their precious baby up above it all.

They circumvent God's law of sowing and reaping and their prodigal never comes to his senses. Instead of allowing him to live with the consequences, the parents live with the bad choices their child is making.

"But he's my baby!" the mother cries.

You must see that before he is your child, he is God's child. Your prodigal is God's baby. Whom do you think your child is hurting the most in his rebellion? The One who loves him the most, God, is being hurt the most. Don't be so preoccupied with how your rebellious child is hurting you; Try to see how he is hurting God.

There is something about living with the consequences of choices that gives us a sharp view of reality. The prodigal son's father let him get to that pig pen and stay there. The stench of those hogs was like spiritual smelling salts to him. It brought him around.

"He finally came to his senses," the Scripture says in Luke 15:17. This shows us that earlier, before his rebellion, his father had planted truth in his son. He knew right from wrong and he knew the way back home.

Because his father had invested God's word into his son, he had hope for his homecoming. He had a promise from God's word that said, "Train up a child in the way he should go, and when he is old he will not depart from it." (Proverbs 22:6 NIV) Perhaps he repeated that promise over and over to himself as he waited day after day, "...When he is old, he will not depart from it...when he is old, he will not depart from it...."

Many have to hold on fiercely to this promise from God. Not every child rebels, but many want to try the way of the world.

Because the prodigal son came to himself, it shows that he was not his true self when he was in rebellion. He was escaping the reality that his father had instilled in him, the foundation of his life. But the deception came to an end as he lived with the consequences of his choices and he returned to the truth. He saw his father for the first time as he really was. He realized his father was loving and reasonable. And he knew he could go home.

If your child is in rebellion, make sure he knows he can come back. Leave a way open for him. Don't fall into that trap of anger, telling him you never want to see him again. If you do, Satan will play that back over and over to him, and God's rescue plans for him can be thwarted.

When the prodigal son walked home, his father saw him coming from a long way off.

I believe there are two reasons for this: First, he was a mess. He had been keeping company with pigs. Maybe his father smelled him coming from a long way off. Secondly, his father had never given up. No doubt he went out to that road every day his son was away and scanned the horizon, watching for him.

When he finally saw him coming one day, what did he do? Did he run out and reprove him? "See what happened, stupid? I told you you'd blow it and waste your money! Your old man isn't as stupid as you thought, is he?"

No. That father wasn't filled with pride; he was filled with the love of God. He didn't drag up the past, he didn't beat his son over the head with all the bad things he had done. Instead, he wept and said, "My son was lost and now he is found!"

In order for there to be hope for a homecoming, you need to have this attitude: say to your son or daughter, "When you want to get out, when you want to change, there's a way out. We'll be waiting for you."

Of course, you will be doing more than waiting. You will be praying, asking God to do whatever it takes to bring your prodigal back to himself.

16
How To Pray
For A Rebel

PERHAPS the thing a rebel needs most is often the most difficult - PRAYER! I am reminded of the young teenager who aspired to become a minister. In his zeal he once approached an older successful preacher of a large church and asked, "What should I do to be sure I am called into the ministry?" To which the old preacher responded, "There are three things you must do. The first one is pray, the second one is pray, and the third one is pray." Prayer is often referred to as the exercise of grandmothers and old ladies who are unable to do little else of significance. Yet I am certain that the power of darkness fears nothing as much as the prayers of godly parents. Often I have heard people say, "Well I guess the only thing we can do is pray," as though somehow prayer is some little pacifier which we may suck on for consolation, but never realize it's benefits. Perhaps this is because only in the last few years have we seen prayer as something that is aggressive (or militant) and not just passive. There are six specific things I would encourage every parent to pray. I'm sure there are others but these are six I would like to concentrate on.

Realize that your rebellious child is, first and foremost, God's child and is hurting Him far more than he is hurting you.

Often the thing that drives us to God in prayer is the grief and pain our child has caused us. Ask God to give you His heart for your child that you might be able to pray His heart for them.

Humble yourself and ask God to show you any attitudes that are causing you to pray selfishly.

Prayers such as, "God, my daughter is pregnant, save her so that she will not be an embarrassment to me and our family," or "God, my son is on drugs, change him so we will not be ashamed to speak of him." I have seen the disappointment of parents who have planned their children's future only to discover that their child had other ambitions genuinely placed in their heart by God. These parents often continue selfishly praying, "Oh God let him be a lawyer like his father," or "Let her marry a preacher." As parents we must symbolically lay our children on the altar of God as Abraham did with Isaac, and pray "God, though you gave this child to me, he is really yours, not mine, your will be done in his life."

Pray they will get caught!

I have seen this particular prayer have tremendous results. I will never forget a 13-year-old I prayed with. I began praying by saying, "Lord, you love this child and your word says 'those who you love you chasten.' I pray now that if he does anything in disobedience to you or his parents, if no one else gets caught that may be involved, I pray he does." A couple of weeks later the boy was told by his mother not to take this bicycle past a certain intersection. The first time he disobeyed his mother, their next door neighbor happened to be driving by the intersection, and drove home and immediately told his mother. Upon being confronted about his disobedience the child said, "I knew I would get caught, ever since that speaker prayed with me, I've been caught every time I do the smallest thing wrong." What a joy when our children begin to experience the chastening of the Lord in every act of disobedience. This is teaching them that even though they are not always under your supervision they are always under God's.

Pray a hedge of protection about them.

Job 1:10 states that God placed a hedge about Job, his house (this included his children) and all that he had. This hedge kept Satan from touching them. In the story we are never told that Job's children are righteous, but because of Job's righteousness, the enemy was not able to harm or destroy them. This of course is his ultimate desire as stated in John 10:10, "The thief comes only in order to steal, kill and destroy." Here some may disagree with me and feel if the children are not living righteously that they will suffer the consequences of their sin. I agree with this but feel that by praying a hedge about your children you are saying "devil you cannot destroy them because they have been committed to God and the hedge God has placed about me includes my house and all I have." This places on parents a great responsibility to live righteously.

Pull down the spiritual strongholds in the lives of your children.

Many people fail to realize that we are involved in spiritual warfare. When Satan fell from heaven one third of the angels fell with him. This angelic army is now a force of spirits without bodies. They are spirits of rebellion, lust, hate, fear, depression etc....They are influencing and ruling the lives of many who are unaware of their presence. Like the classic movie, *The Invisible Man* their strength is in the fact that they are not seen. Therefore to ignore them simply gives them greater strength. Eph. 6:12 states "For we are not fighting against people made of flesh and blood, but against persons without bodies the evil rulers of the unseen world, those mighty satanic beings and great evil princes of darkness who rule this world: and against huge numbers of wicked spirits in the spirit world." (*The Living Bible*).

As a parent it is often very difficult not to take the rebellion of your children personally. When we take it as a personal attack from our children we are fighting against flesh and blood. After prayer, identify to the best of your ability the spirits controlling or influencing your child; then in prayer begin to address or speak to that spirit or spirits. For example, "You spirit of lust that is influencing my child, I speak to you in the name of Jesus, to let go of my son or daughter. I declare war on you. You cannot continue to control them." This should be a daily exercise until you begin to see them free from the control of that spirit. Remember Jesus looking at Peter and boldly saying, "Get thee behind me Satan." Jesus realized that the spirit influencing Peter at the time was that of the devil, not Peter himself. Rather than addressing Peter, He spoke to the spirit. We must do the same. I remember hearing of a godly mother who once declared "Satan, I know my son is in rebellion and on drugs. And if it is a fight between his will and God's will, that's one thing. But if it's a fight between your will and his will, I'm going to battle in prayer Satan, and I will not come out a loser." Today her son is one of America's greatest Bible teachers.

Some may question "Do we really have this type of authority as Christians?" Listen to the exhortation of the Apostle Paul to the Corinthians.

> I hope I won't need to show you when I come how harsh and rough I can be. I don't want to carry out my present plans against some of you who seem to think my deeds and words are merely those of an ordinary man. It is true that I am an ordinary, weak human being, but I don't use human plans and methods to win my battles. I use God's mighty

weapons, not those made by men, to knock down the devil's strongholds. These weapons can break down every proud argument against God and every wall that can be built to keep from finding Him. With these weapons I can capture rebels and bring them back to God, and change them into men whose hearts desire is obedience to Christ. I will use these weapons against every rebel who remains after I have first used them on you yourselves, and you surrender to Christ.

(2 Cor. 102-6, *The Living Bible*)

As a Christian parent you can never over-emphasize the effect of prayer and fasting in pulling down the satanic influences affecting your children.

Pray God will lead other believers across your child's path.

A few years ago there seemed to be a surplus of books written on angels. One author even claimed to be visited on a number of occasions by angels. After reading the book I was inclined to believe he had experienced angelic visitations. One particular story he shared of a conversation with an angel moved me greatly. The angel shared with him that every time we began to pray for someone, angels are immediately charged by God to go and prepare circumstances to bring someone across the path of the person we are praying for. I have talked to many parents who have seen this at work. One mother prayed that God would touch her rebellious son who was thousands of miles away in the army. One night while on his way to party, as he walked through the streets of San Francisco, he heard a street preacher. Convicted by the Holy Spirit he called out to Christ. His circumstances had been ordered by the Lord and a praying mother. On another occasion I served as chaplin for a college basketball team. The coach was very excited about a new player he had recruited from New York. The beginning of basketball work-outs was my first opportunity to speak to the team. As the coach introduced me, the player from New York yelled out "Oh no, I moved away from New York to get away from all this God stuff, my Mom is always preaching to me." Though he had moved out of the influence of his Mom, he was not out of the influence of her prayers.

17

SEVEN PRODIGALS

OR

IT'S NEVER TOO LATE

WHEN you're waiting at the end of the road for your prodigal to come home, it may help to hear the words of some parents who have been there and have seen God bring total victory.

Two such parents are my father-and mother-in-law. I would like to share a conversation I had with them. I asked them to reveal their spiritual struggles with seven prodigal children. The principles they learned were hard-won, but practical and powerful.

Brian and Louise had been married for 18 years when they met Christ; their two oldest children were in high school. Each one of their seven rebelled against them and against God. One was into drugs, hanging around with a motorcycle gang. Another was living an immoral life, and another ran away from home. The other four were "compliant rebels," going to church but also sneaking off to bars and such.

That was many years ago. One by one, each of their seven prodigals returned. Here is their story.

Jacob: "Louise, what was the difference in the character of your children from one another?"

Louise: "One thing we never did—even before we came to know the Lord—was to compare our children to each other. Somehow we realized each was unique; each had good qualities and each had things he or she needed to work on. We treated them as individuals and met them right where they were.

"Since coming to the Lord, we've realized that's how God treats us. He meets each of us right where we are.

"God gave us that principle even before we knew His Word. Each child was different...some were independent, some were shy, some were outgoing, some were dependent. We treated each one differently. That's one reason our children always enjoyed each other's company. They didn't have to compete with each other or try to be someone else."

Brian: "Our oldest son, our second-born, wrote us a letter recently. He said he was thankful for the special attention we had always given him. He said we had always made each one feel like he or she was our favorite.

"You know, that's what God does for us. We're each so special to Him that Jesus would have died for only one of us if only one had sinned. He doesn't prefer one of us over the other—we're all the same in His eyes."

Jacob: "The Bible says not to compare yourselves among yourselves. One person said if you do and you feel like you're less than the other person, you will feel condemned; if you feel equal to the one you're comparing yourself to, you'll feel competitive; if you feel greater, you'll become proud."

Brian: "There was a gap between our first two children and the latter five. Our oldest, a girl, and our oldest son grew up when my wife and I were rebels ourselves—rebels away from

109

God. They saw that and based their lives on it. But when we came to the Lord, the spiritual condition of our home changed. By then the older two were moving out on their own.

"The younger ones, however, were raised in a new spiritual environment. They were brought up in the things of the Lord, and saw a completely different mother and father."

Jacob: "Each of the seven rebelled. Were the reactions of each one different?"

Louise: "Jacob, when we say all rebelled, we do not mean they were all outwardly rebellious."

Brian: "The two older ones were raised with no mercy or grace—only the law we laid down."

Jacob: "Rules without relationship?"

Brian: "Yes. The older two seemed fine. But their rebellion manifested itself after they left home.

"But with the younger five, where we had more relationship, there was open rebellion. God showed us how to deal with each one differently."

Jacob: "Charles Stanley said, 'By listening to your kids today, you earn the right to be heard tomorrow.' Most kids go through a rebellious stage. If you have enough relationship built ahead of time, there's a bridge between you and them and you can communicate even while they're going through that."

Louise: "There was no bridge with the older two."

Jacob: "Some who will be reading this interview will wonder, 'What do I do if I come to the Lord and my children are already in their teens and they've established their habit patterns?'

110

How did you folks treat your older children?"

Brian: "We wondered what to do. They were about to graduate from high school. They had seen all the inconsistencies and rebellion in our lives before we came to the Lord. How could we now start doing what was right and telling them to do something we hadn't been doing ourselves until now?

"One Scripture we always stood on was Romans 8:28, 'All things work together for good to those who love God, to those who are called according to His purpose.' We knew we had been called to raise our family for Christ. We knew God wasn't going to let that rebellious situation that existed before we were saved go on uncorrected.

"We also knew He'd move in the situation because we kept it before Him in prayer. We kept our home in a spiritual state—not some hyper-spirituality, but the real thing. That's what the children saw. One thing that breeds rebellion is when kids see anything that's false. But when Louise and I came to the Lord it was a real conversion. Our kids saw us in a real daily walk with the Lord. They saw the change in our lives.

"After much prayer—prayer, prayer and more prayer—we began explaining things to the older children. Because they could see the change in us, it wasn't hard to sit down and explain the Gospel to them. We told them how we felt differently about things now that we knew the Lord."

Louise: "Another Scripture we stood on for all seven children was Phil. 1:6, 'He who has begun a good work in you will perform it until the day of Jesus Christ.'

"The younger five were raised in a Bible-believing church and knew all the language, going through all the motions for years. When they started into rebellion, it was much easier to deal with because of the conviction of the Holy Spirit. It was easier to reason with them because they knew the truth.

"We always had an expectancy in the house...we always

knew that God would answer our prayers. We lived waiting for them to change, waiting for God to work in their lives. Because of that expectancy, we used every opportunity given to us to minister to our children."

Jacob: "What were the different ways each rebelled? Didn't you have one who was deceptive, with hidden rebellion, while another was more open? Weren't some quiet and laid back while others were vocal and defiant?"

Louise: "Yes. But the main thing was, when they were going through their rebellion, they always knew Brian was the head of our home. They had that security. They also knew that even though we loved them, there were things we wouldn't tolerate. The things of the Lord were serious with us. Brian never made light of sin."

Brian: "Even before Louise and I knew the Lord, we had a reverence for the home—we were raised to hold home in high esteem. That gave us a background for how to react when rebellion surfaced. Then when we came to Jesus, we had even more insight on how to handle it."

Louise: "We dealt with each situation as it arose. We never put it aside until the next day, but dealt with it immediately."

Brian: "Even though each situation was different, it was a natural thing for us to deal with because we felt God equipping us each time. When we felt we were at our wits' end, worrying that maybe we were saying the wrong things or coming on too strong, we'd always put it in the Lord's hands one more time. We said, 'Lord, if we've blown it, we count on you to take care of it.' "

Louise: "We were never our children's friends—never just their buddies. We were always their parents. Children have

112

enough friends, but they only have one set of parents."

Jacob: "How did they come to the Lord?"

Louise: "The one who came first was the one we thought would be the last—our second born, our oldest son. Now we know, the more hungry you are and the more you're seeking, the more you're outwardly rebellious. The one speaking the loudest is the one that's often the most in need. But we didn't know that then."

Jacob: "The first to come to the Lord was your oldest son— one of the two raised when you weren't Christians. Wasn't that a gift of grace to you from the Lord? A lot of people think they have to suffer through some kind of penance. But I've found there's more grace for situations we got into before we were saved. God holds you more accountable after you come to know Him."

Louise: "We were so concerned about him. God took him 2,000 miles away, in the armed services. I later realized it was easier for us to pray for him that way—we didn't have to face what he was involved in every day. We just prayed.

"Every day I lined my children up before the throne of God in my mind's eye as I prayed. I called each one by name, presenting them to the Lord. One night while I was doing this, it was as though I had a vision. Jesus stepped down from the throne and came and took my oldest son by the hand. He led him back to the throne to the Father.

"I knew then—he was going to come. I shared this with Brian and we kept that fresh in our minds. And it wasn't long until he was saved."

Brian: "I was concerned also about our firstborn, our eldest daughter. I thought God was going to have to knock her off her horse like Saul on the road to Damascus. She was so independent as well as being rebellious."

Jacob: "Let me bring this out. Your oldest child manifested rebellion through independence, but the second showed withdrawal. Yet both were in rebellion."

Brian: "That's right. We considered the chances of our daughter coming to the Lord to be as remote as our son, but we were in for a surprise with her, too. She just came 'waltzing in'! She was the last of the seven, but in her time, she came easily."

Jacob: "Your oldest son was thousands of miles away and walked by as a street preacher was preaching. He listened and God took the seed you all had planted, and a street preacher none of you knew led your son to the Lord.

"I think it's important to realize that just because your child is physically away from you doesn't mean he or she is out of the reach of God. And isn't it something that your son had the Damascus Road type conversion, whereas your daughter had more of a gradual turning to God?"

Jacob: "What about the younger five?"

Brian: "We had to deal totally differently with them than with the older two. The first two were grown and out of our reach. All we could do was get on our knees before God and believe He was going to move in their lives.

"But these younger ones were still in the home and we had to discipline them. In some cases, it meant the rod—even though they were a little old for that. We didn't believe we should stand for children who were not only disobedient, but unruly."

Jacob: "With Michelle (who would later be my wife), you dealt drastically differently. (As I recall the story, she was 16 and had run away from home). You went and found her, then flew her 500 miles away, dropping her at a Christian ministry. With the older two, you abandoned them to God, but with Michelle, you pulled her out of the fire."

Brian: "Even though that rebellion surfaced, we wouldn't tolerate it. We had to deal with it. With Michelle, and with each of the others, God always provided the means we were to use. As we sought God and godly counsel from others, we always got specific directions."

Jacob: "I've seen some parents at a crisis point who wouldn't do what you did with Michelle. They say, 'Well, she's 16...almost an adult. If that's what she wants to do, let her do it.' Yet, you took pretty bold action."

Brian: "Whenever Louise and I acted in times of crisis, we had perfect peace from God that we were doing the right thing. We never lost control of ourselves."

Jacob: "When things were out of control, you didn't lose peace because you knew God was really in control of the situation."

Louise: "Brian and I are not always in agreement. But in times of crisis, we come together in total agreement. We don't blame one another for the situation. "

Jacob: "That's the key. Often during a crisis, parents disagree. There isn't unity so the situation worsens. I remember your saying that during those days, you'd get up in the middle of the night and find Brian on the bathroom floor, crying out to God for your children. So it's more than just trusting God, or taking appropriate action. There was lots of prayer and fasting, wasn't there?"

Louise: "I'm so grateful that Brian put in those hours praying. I've gone to bed at night with a rebellious child and awakened the next morning to a kid with an entirely different attitude. And it's because of those hours Brian spent in prayer. That's the most important thing—praying for your children. That's spiritual warfare.

"When we made that decision to send Michelle away, we had lots of people against us. Our immediate family and church people disagreed with our actions."

Jacob: "You even pulled her out of high school, didn't you?"

Louise: "That's right, and nobody understood. But Brian and I were in agreement and knew what we had to do. It was the turning point of Michelle's life.

"I've seen parents in similar situations, going back and forth in their reactions. They know what they're supposed to do, but they're afraid of what people think, or afraid of their children's reactions.

"When God leads you in a certain direction, if you've spent time with Him and know He is telling you to do it, then do it— no matter what! If you've heard from Him and have had godly counsel, just do it. God will work it out."

Jacob: "What one or two key things did you hold on to while waiting for your children to come back from their rebellion?"

Brian: "Trusting God was the first thing. We trusted God and turned it over to Him completely. Many times we were so close either to a breakthrough or to losing it all. All we could do was trust Him. There were volatile situations.

"Also, God has blessed Louise with a gift for reasoning with her children. She could sit them down and reason with them. They respected her and had enough godly covering over them to realize what she was saying was true. They couldn't deny the love we both had for them. It broke through all their

116

hardness and the Holy Spirit cracked the shell."

Louise: "I think the children knew we had their best interests at heart. Children know. They have more discernment than most adults. They know if you're sincere and really love them and if you've sacrificed your life for them."

Brian: "We held onto Philippians 1:6 and Romans 8:28 and many other Scriptures which God quickened to us for what we were going through. We had a lot of faith in God's Word."

Today, all seven of Louise and Brian's children are living for the Lord. One is my wife, Michelle. Four others are in full-time Christian ministry. The older two are active in their local churches.

18

THE WISDOM OF PARENTS: TRAINING CHILDREN WHO ARE NOT REBELLIOUS

MANY times while speaking to parents in seminars I ask, "If you plant corn in good fertile ground, what do you get?"

"Corn!" is the resounding answer.

"What do you get if you plant rice in good fertile ground?" I question.

"Rice." comes the reply.

"Well, what do you get if you plant nothing in good fertile ground?"

Some may say "Nothing," but then they stop and think.

Ask any farmer. Take good fertile ground and plant nothing in it and in no time at all, you'll have weeds. The same is true when it comes to training your children.

God gave us children so that we could cultivate good things in them, bringing them up in the nurture and admonition of the Lord. (Eph. 6:4 KJV)

Catherine Booth, wife of Salvation Army founder, General William Booth, wrote about what this kind of training means.

Nurture means nursing, feeding, strengthening, developing. Admonition means reproof, caution, instruction.

Here is the order of God. Firstly, the feeding and strengthening of all that is good in them; and secondly, the reproof and caution against evil; and thirdly, instruction in righteousness. [44]

It is so important to include both nurturing and admonition. The whole reason God invented families, with small dependent beings given to adults, was to give us greater understanding of Him and His love for us.

As John Dawson says in his pamphlet, *The Father Heart of God*, the Lord could easily have come up with a reproductive system that produced physically completed persons, such as His original creation of Adam and Eve.

Instead, He created the family as a circle of relationship, including an adult male and female into which tiny, helpless human beings are born and raised. Even our relatively slow growth and maturation rate, compared to other mammals, underscores this. God wants us to come into the world totally dependent and helpless, because He intends the family unit to be a place where His love is demonstrated to both parent and child.

As they raise children, parents learn God's heart towards us as His children. And as children, it is God's will for us to see His love revealed through parental care and training.

But too often even Christian parents confuse "training" with "teaching." They spend their time giving children knowledge instead of instilling values in them.

William and Catherine Booth raised many children and saw all of them end up as workers in God's Kingdom, taking the Gospel to many nations, including India, France, Switzerland, and the United States.

With such a track record, we can listen to this mother's advice and accumulated wisdom. Catherine Booth wrote:

119

Christian parents so often forget whose their children are....settle it in your minds that your child belongs absolutely to God and not to you— that you are only stewards for God, holding your children to nurse them and train them for Him.

The training God requires is a *moral training* (emphasis mine)—the inspiring of the child with the love of goodness, truth, and righteousness, and leading him to its practice and exercise in all the duties and emergencies of life.

Train...does not mean merely to teach. Some parents...cram [their children] with religious sentiment and truth, making them commit to memory the Catechism, large portions of Scripture, a great many hymns, and so on....which may all be done without a single stroke of real training such as God requires, and such as the hearts of our children need. Nay, this mere teaching, informing the head without interesting or influencing the heart, frequently drives children off from God and goodness, and makes them hate, instead of love, everything connected with religion.

Suppose..that you have a vine, and that this vine is endowed with reason, and will, and moral sense. You say to your vine-dresser, "Now, I want that vine trained,"—i.e., made to grow in a particular way....Suppose your vine-dresser goes to your vine every morning, and says to it, "Now, you must let that branch grow in this direction, and that branch grow in another; you are not to put forth too many shoots here, nor too many tendrils there; you must not waste your sap in too many leaves;" and having told it what to do and how to grow, he shuts it up and leaves it to itself. This is precisely the way many good people act towards their children.

[Such parents] teach what they neither practice

themselves nor take the trouble to see that their children practice, and the children see through the hollow sham, and learn to despise both their parents and their religion. Mother, if you want to train your child you must practice what you teach, and you must show him how to practice it also, and you must, at all costs of trouble and care, see that he does it.

To secure obedience...you must begin early enough. This is where multitudes of mothers miss their mark; they begin too late. The great majority of children are ruined for the formation of character before they are five years old by the foolish indulgence of mothers.

There is a way of speaking to and handling an infant compatible with the utmost love and tenderness, which teaches it that mother is not to be trifled with; that, although she loves and caresses, she is to be obeyed, and will be obeyed, and a child that is trained in this way will not, as a rule, attempt to resist.

I have proved it, I think, with some as strong-willed children as ever came into the world. I conquered them at six and ten months old, and seldom had to contend with any direct opposition after.

Perhaps there are some mothers who are saying, "Ah, I see it now; but it is too late...." I say: Better late than never. Begin and do all you can. Perhaps you can never undo all the mischief, but you may a part of it. Call your children around you; confess your past unfaithfulness in your dealings with them, fall on your knees before the Lord with them, and tell Him of your failure to train them for Him, and ask His help to enable you to do it in the future. When you rise from your knees tell your children in the most solemn manner that you see your mistake, and feel how awful it would be, if they were to be lost through your fault, and that from this hour you are going to be obeyed in everything. Begin at once to exact obedience. Be judicious and forbearing, remembering that your children's habits of disobedience are the result of your own folly, and deal as gently as the case will permit; but at all costs secure obedience, and never more allow your commands to be trifled with.

Do not be afraid to use your authority. One would think...some parents...did not possess an iota of power over [their children]. All they dare to do, seems to be to reason, to persuade, to coax. I have frequently heard mothers using all manner of persuasion instead of exerting the authority which God has given for the safeguard and guidance of their poor children.

They give their commands in such a voice as leaves it optional whether the child shall obey them or not, and this he understands very well; there is no command, no firmness, no decision, no authority, and the child knows it by its instincts just as an animal would. Men are much wiser in breaking in and training their horses than their sons, hence they generally are much better served by the former than the latter!

Eli, [received] one of the most terrible strokes of vengeance recorded in the whole Bible. What was it for? Not for using profane language before his children, not for training them in unrighteousness or immorality, for he was a good and righteous man, but "because he restrained them not." That means he did not use his authority on the side of God and righteousness....

What a contrast...[with] the conduct of Abraham! "I know him," said Jehovah, "that he will command his children and his household after him." Not merely remonstrate, persuade, and threaten, as Eli did, but *command*....Parents, if you fulfill your part of the covenant, never fear but that God will perform His. Only you train your children truly for Him, and He will charge Himself with their future.... [45]

Isn't it amazing how up-to-date Catherine Booth's advice is, written at the turn of the last century, even as we are about to enter a new century?

Other parents with good advice to give are two missionaries I met while in Africa.

Don and Sue Myers are the directors of African Affairs with Campus Crusade for Christ in Kenya. All five of their children are working in some part of the world as missionaries with Campus Crusade. I was so challenged by Don and Sue, hearing how God had worked mightily in their children, calling each in unique ways.

Don wasn't always a Christian. He was saved at age 33 after most of the children were already born. Yet God restored all that the enemy had destroyed. Don and Sue's testimony is, "It's never too late!"

I asked Don for any principles to share with other parents that were consistent in their family while raising their children. He gave me five:

Holy Heroes

Don and Sue were often visited in their home by other ministers. They took these opportunities to stress to their children the importance of serving God and sharing friendship with godly individuals. These people who were honored by their parents also became the children's heroes. As the Meyers family elevated the office of full-time service to God, small seeds were being planted in their children's hearts to become like those they admired the most. Parents, who do you elevate before your children and most admire?

Dedicated Discipline

Don stressed the word "dedicated" because discipline cannot be merely a stage in raising children. Parents must dedicate themselves to the practice of it.

Don smiled and said, "Believe me, you will have plenty of practice!"

Persevering Prayer

Prayer for our children is often based upon immediate needs for their attitudes and well-being. But Don shared how he and Sue had been praying for the future mates of each of their children since they were little. He then grinned proudly as only a grandfather can and said, "Now they are praying for the mates of our grandchildren."

Making Memories

As missionaries, the Meyers lived on a very restricted budget. Many times this limited the material things they could give their children. Yet Don says now their grown children's most pleasant memories are of those cheap picnics when they flew kites and ran in the park. Other fond memories were of the family devotions that Don led. All of these were not expensive financially but often very costly in time.

Quality Cues

Don stresses that we need to see quality time from our children's perspective. Many times what we consider quality time and what our children consider quality time are two different things. For a 3-year-old, quality time may be 30 minutes of your playing in the sand with him. For a 5-year-old, it may mean 30 minutes of reading her favorite book to her. To a teenaged boy, it could mean an afternoon of hunting. Let your child give you the cue of what quality time is to him. This will always be changing as he grows and matures.

124

Don and Sue summed up their advice by saying that the reason all their children were serving God in such a wonderful way was because of the grace of God.

If we follow this godly counsel we will be training our children not to be rebels but effective servants of the Lord Jesus.

A Final Word To Fathers

Someone once said, "If you want to know who God most desires to use, look at who the devil is most attacking." If this is true, and I believe it is, then it is easy to see that you as a father have been under attack. The devil is not only trying to destroy you as an individual, but also your office as a father. Fathers are in greater demand today than they have ever been in history.

> In the 60s we lost the Family
> In the 70s we lost Authority
> In the 80s we lost Love
> In the 90s we are losing Hope

All of this began with the loss of the family (namely fathers through adultery and divorce). In homes where the father is no longer present, the children are left with an improper understanding of authority. Women now assume the responsibilities that should naturally be assumed by the father.

As a father myself, my greatest goal in life is for my children to grow up and be able to say, "The most godly, responsible person I know is my Dad." Recently, in a hunting blind, I began talking about the importance of my relationship with God, my wife, and my children to the vice-president of one of the largest companies in America. After a few moments of silence, he looked at me and said, "Why didn't anyone tell me this before it was too late?"

Most children are born when their fathers are between twenty and forty years old. During this time most fathers are working hard to establish themselves in their careers. This is when most men are at their peak earning power. When they are finally secure in their career they realize that this is not nearly as important or fulfilling as they thought it would be. They then direct their energy toward what is left of their relationships with their wives and children. It is at this time they discover that Mom and the kids have adapted to a life without Dad who is now an awkward intruder.

Fathers: never forget that your children develop their views of God (their heavenly Father) from their views of you (their earthly father). This places a tremendous responsibility upon you. My prayer for you is that your children will be able to see God in your love, patience, forgiveness, discipline, and hope for them. Remember Dad, God exercises these attitudes toward you. The miracle of Christian life is that we can see a perfect God even in imperfect people. God never asks us to do anything that he doesn't give us both the power and ability by his grace to do. So from one father to another, go out and make some child want to grow up and be just like you. Because after all, they will.

A Final Word To Mothers

Mothers, your importance and role in the family is irreplaceable. As most fathers have neglected their responsibilities to the family to be anything other than provider, mothers have been by and large the glue that holds most families together. The call to a career and fulfillment outside the home is a constant battle you will have to fight. Single mothers and some two-parent families have no choice in this matter. For them the goal of just providing for their family necessitates them working. Sadly enough just being a mother and homemaker is not very esteemed in our culture. Yet any casual observer can see we are suffering as a society because we have the first generation of teenagers who for the most part have raised themselves. Some have even borne the responsibility of raising their younger brothers and sisters. It is not uncommon to see some teenagers raising their parents.

I applaud every mother who has chosen to make the priority of her life the raising of godly children. I am reminded of Catherine Booth, co-founder of the Salvation Army, who once said to her children while putting them to sleep, "Sleep on my child; the world is waiting for you." How right she was. They were all world-changers. Why? Because of a godly mother's investment! If I were to place an ad in the newspaper recruiting mothers it would read like this:

> WANTED
> Female who is willing to:
> Be on call 24 hours
> Be a short order and gourmet cook
> Clean house, vacuum and do windows
> Do after school tutoring
> Wash, dry, iron and sew clothes
> Have interior decorating experience
> Hospital and Nursing experience helpful
> Must be a good driver
> Be cordial Hostess and entertainer
> Must be attractive, polite and well-dressed at all times
>
> Few Benefits for the first twenty years. No guaranteed pay. The job is rough but the rewards are eternal.

128

NOTES

1. *Statistical Abstract of the United States 1987* (Washington D.C.: U.S. Department of Commerce, Bureau of the Census, 1987).

2. Ibid.

3. Adele Greenfield, "The Ordeal of Battered Parents," *American Way*, 1 November 1986.

4. Patrick Buchanan, "Fight the Swedenization of America," *Los Angeles Times-Examiner*, 28 June 1989.

5. *The Southeast Christian Witness*, November 1986.

6. Dawson McAllister, *A Heart for Reaching Lost America* (audio cassette) (Columbia, Tennessee: Shepherd Productions).

7. Greenfield, "The Ordeal of Battered Parents."

8. Winkie Pratney, *Devil Take the Youngest* (Shreveport, Louisiana: Huntington House, 1985).

9. Ibid.

10. James Dobson, *Turn Your Heart Toward Home* (video cassette) (Waco, Texas: Word, Inc.).

11. Teenage Research Unlimited, Syndicated Study, 1986.

12. James Dobson, *What Wives Wish Their Husbands Knew About Women*, (Wheaton, Illinois: Tyndale House Publishers, 1981).

13. Armand M. Nicholi, Jr., M.D., "Changes in the American Family: Their Impact on Individual Development and on Society," (unpublished typescript, n.d.).

14. *USA Today*, 14 June 1989.

15. Josh McDowell, *Understanding Youth Today* (video cassette) (Dallas, Texas: Josh McDowell Ministry).

16. Ibid.

17. Pratney, *Devil Take the Youngest*.

18. "Today's Adolescents—Different Choices, Greater Risks," *Youthworker Update*, February 1987.

19. Dorriet Kavanaugh, ed., *Listen To Us! The Children's Express Report* (New York: Workman Publishing, 1978).

20. Linda S. Lichter, Robert Lichter, and Stanley Rothman, "Lichter/Rothman Survey," *Public Opinion*, [?] 1985.

21. "Perils Cited for Latchkey Children," *Youthletter*, March 1986.

22. Ibid.

23. Gary Bauer, *Presidential Report on the Family*.

24. Nicholi, "Changes in the American Family."

25. Ibid.

26. "Report on Working Mothers," *Family Research Today*, 10 September 1985.

27. Wallerstein and Kelly study, 1980.

28. David Wilkerson, *Sippin' Saints* (Old Tappen, New Jersey: Spire Books, 1979).

29. Ibid.

30. *Encyclopedia Brittanica*, 11th ed., s.v. "alcoholism."

31. McDowell, *Understanding Youth Today* (video cassette).

32. Ibid.

33. Geraldine Youcha and Judith Seixas, "Drinking, Drugs and Your Child," *Parents*, March 1989.

34. Donald P. Orr and Maureen C. Downes, "Self-Concept of Adolescent Sexual Abuse Victims," *Journal of Youth and Adolescence*, October 1985.

35. McDowell, *Understanding Youth Today* (video casette)

36. Warren W. Wiersbe, *What To Do About Teenage Rebellion* (pamphlet) (Success With Youth Publications).

37. Dudley Hall, *Delightful or Delinquent Children: Notes on Discipline* (pamphlet) (Euless, Texas: Successful Christian Living Ministries).

38. Winkie Pratney, "Hurt and Bitterness" (tract, reproduced from *Last Days Magazine*) (Lindale, Texas: Last Days Ministries).

39. Diane Salvatore, "Teen Rage," *Ladies Home Journal*, February 1987.

40. Greenfield, "The Ordeal of Battered Parents."

41. Pratney, *Devil Take the Youngest*.

42. "Teen Rage," *Ladies Home Journal*.

43. "Today's Adolescents..." *Youthworker Update*.

44. Catherine Booth, *Practical Religion* (Atlanta, Georgia: Salvation Army Supplies, 1986).

45. Ibid.

REFERENCE BIBLES

(A.V.)   *The Amplified Bible*. Grand Rapids, Michigan: Zondervan Bible Publishers, 1985.

(KJV)   *The King James Version*. Wheaton, Illinois: Tyndale House Publishers, 1983.

(NASB) *New American Standard Bible*. Iowa Falls, Iowa: Riverside/World Publishing, 1987.

(NIV)   *New International Version of the Holy Bible*. Grand Rapids, Michigan: Zondervan Bible Publishers.

(NKJ)   *New King James Version*. Nashville, Tennessee: Thomas Nelson, Inc., Publishers.

The Living Bible. Wheaton, Illinois: Tyndale House Publishers, 1983.

More Good Books From Huntington House Publishers

Kinsey, Sex and Fraud: The Indoctrination of a People
by Dr. Judith A. Reisman and Edward Eichel

Kinsey, Sex and Fraud describes the research of Alfred Kinsey which shaped Western society's beliefs and understanding of the nature of human sexuality. His unchallenged conclusions are taught at every level of education—elementary, highschool and college—and quoted in textbooks as undisputed truth.

The authors clearly demonstrate that Kinsey's research involved illegal experimentations on several hundred children. The survey was carried out on a non-representative group of Americans, including disproportionately large numbers of sex offenders, prostitutes, prison inmates and exhibitionists.

ISBN 0-910311-20-X $19.95 Hard cover

Seduction of the Innocent Revisited by John Fulce

You honestly can't judge a book by its cover—especially a comic book! Comic books of yesteryear bring to mind cute cartoon characters, super-heroes battling the forces of evil or a sleuth tracking down the bad guy clue-by-clue. But that was a long, long time ago.

Today's comic books aren't innocent at all! Author John Fulce asserts that "super-heroes" are constantly found in the nude engaging in promiscuity, and satanic symbols are abundant throughout the pages. Fulce says most parents aren't aware of the contents of today's comic books—of what their children are absorbing from these seemingly innocent forms of entertainment. As a comic book collector for many years, Fulce opened his own comic book store in 1980, only to sell the business a few short years later due to the steady influx of morally unacceptable material. What's happening in the comic book industry? Fulce outlines the moral, biblical, and legal aspects and proves his assertions with page after page of illustrations. We need to pay attention to what our children are reading, Fulce claims. Comic books are not as innocent as they used to be.

ISBN 0-910311-66-8 $8.95

"Soft Porn" Plays Hardball by Dr. Judith A. Reisman

With amazing clarity, the author demonstrates that pornography imposes on society a view of women and children that encourages violence and sexual abuse. As crimes against women and children increase to alarming proportions, it's of paramount importance that we recognize the cause of this violence. Pornography should be held accountable for the havoc it has wreaked in our homes and our country.

ISBN 0-901311-65-X $ 8.95 Trade paper
ISBN 0-910311-92-7 $16.95 Hardcover

Dinosaurs and the Bible by David W. Unfred

Every reader, young and old, will be fascinated by this ever-mysterious topic—exactly what happened to the dinosaurs? Author David Unfred draws a very descriptive picture of the history and fate of the dinosaurs, using the Bible as a reference guide.

In this educational and informative book, Unfred answers such questions as: Did dinosaurs really exist? Does the Bible mention dinosaurs? What happened to dinosaurs, or are there some still living awaiting discovery? Unfred uses the Bible to help unlock the ancient mysteries of the lumbering creatures, and teaches how those mysteries can educate us about God the Creator and our God of Love.

ISBN 0-910311-70-6 $12.95 Hard cover

God's Rebels by Henry Lee Curry III

From his unique perspective Dr. Henry Lee Curry III offers a fascinating look at the lives of some of our greatest Southern religious leaders during the Civil War. The rampant Evangelical Christianity prominent at the outbreak of the Civil War, asserts Dr. Curry, is directly traceable to the 2nd Great Awakening of the early 1800s. The evangelical tradition, with its emphasis on strict morality, individual salvation, and emotional worship, had influenced most of Southern Protestantism by this time. Southerners unquestionably believed the voice of the ministers to be the "voice of God"; consequently, the church became one of the most powerful forces influencing Confederate life and morale. Inclined toward a Calvinistic emphasis on predestination, the South was confident that God would sustain its way of life.

Dr. Curry illuminates the many different activities in which Confederate clergymen engaged. He focuses on three prominent clergymen in the heart of the South. James A. Duncan, editor of the Richmond Christian Advocate, Moses I. Hoge, Honorary chaplain of the Confederate Congress who ran the Union blockade in order to get Bibles for Confederate soldiers, and Charles F. E. Minnigerods, a pastor of one of the most important parishes in the South.

Dr. Curry is a Virginian. He holds degrees from the University of Virginia, Duke University, and Emory University. While teaching at Mercer University's Atlanta Campus, his course on The Civil War and Reconstruction was always very popular.

ISBN: 0-910311-67-6 $12.95 Trade paper
ISBN: 0-910311-68-4 $21.95 Hard cover

Inside the New Age Nightmare by Randall Baer

Now, for the first time, one of the most powerful and influential leaders of the New Age movement has come out to expose the deceptions of the organization he once led. New Age magazines and articles have for many years hailed Randall Baer as their most "radically original" and "advanced" thinker... "light years ahead of others" says leading New Age magazine *East-West Journal*. His bestselling books on quartz crystals, self-transformation, and planetary ascension have won worldwide acclaim and been extolled by New Agers from all walks of life.

Hear, from a New Age insider, the secret plans they have spawned to take over our public, private, and political institutions. Have these plans already been implemented in your church, business, or organization? Discover the seduction of the demonic forces at work—turned from darkness to light, Randall Baer reveals the methods of the New Age movement as no one else can. Find out what you can do to stop the New Age movement from destroying our way of life.

ISBN 0-910311-58-7 $8.95

The Devil's Web by Pat Pulling with Kathy Cawthon

This explosive exposé presents the first comprehensive guide to childhood and adolescent occult involvement. Written by a nationally recognized occult crime expert, the author explains how the violent occult underworld operates and how they stalk and recruit our children, teenagers and young adults for their evil purposes. The author leaves no stone unturned in her investigation and absolves no one of the responsibility of protecting our children. She dispels myths and raises new questions examining the very real possibility of the existence of major occult networks which may include members of law enforcement, government officials and other powerful individuals.

ISBN 0-910311-59-5 $8.95 Trade paper
ISBN 0-910311-63-3 $16.95 Hard cover

From Rock to Rock by Eric Barger

Over three years in the making, the pages of this book represent thousands of hours of detailed research as well as over twenty-six years of personal experience and study. The author presents a detailed exposé on many current rock entertainers, rock concerts, videos, lyrics and occult symbols used within the industry. He also presents a rating system of over fifteen hundred past and present rock groups and artists.

ISBN 0-910311-61-7 $8.95

The Deadly Deception: Freemasonry Exposed By One of Its Top Leaders by Tom McKenney

Presents a frank look at Freemasonry and its origin. Learn of the "secrets" and "deceptions" that are practiced daily around the world. Find out why Masonry teaches that it is the true religion, that all other religions are but corrupted and perverted forms of Masonry.

ISBN 0-910311-54-4 $7.95

Lord! Why Is My Child a Rebel? by Jacob Aranza

This book offers an analysis of the root causes of teenage rebellion and offers practical solutions for disoriented parents. Aranza focuses on the turbulent teenage years, and how to survive those years—both you and the child! Must reading for parents—especially for those with strong-willed children. This book will help you avoid the traps in which many parents are caught and put you on the road to recovery with your rebel.

ISBN 0-910311-62-5 $6.95

New World Order: The Ancient Plan of Secret Societies by William Still

Secret societies such as Freemasons have been active since before the advent of Christ, yet most of us don't realize what they are or the impact they've had on many historical events. For example, did you know secret societies played a direct role in the French Revolutions of the 18th and 19th centuries and the Russian Revolution of the 20th century? Author William Still brings into focus the actual manipulative work of the societies, and the "Great Plan" they follow, much to the surprise of many of those who are blindly led into the organization. Their ultimate goal is simple: world dictatorship and unification of all mankind into a world confederation.

Most Masons are good, decent men who join for fellowship, but they are deceived—pulled away from their religious heritage. Only those who reach the highest level of the Masons know its true intentions. Masons and Marxists follow the same master. Ultimately it is a struggle between two foes—the forces of religion versus the forces of anti-religion. Still asserts that although the final battle is near-at-hand, the average person has the power to thwart the efforts of secret societies. Startling and daring, this is the first successful attempt by an author to unveil the designs of secret societies from the beginning, up to the present and into the future. The author attempts to educate the community on how to recognize the signals and how to take the necessary steps to impede their progress.

ISBN 0-910311-64-1 $8.95

Hidden Dangers of the Rainbow by Constance Cumbey
The first book to uncover and expose the New Age movement, this national #1 bestseller paved the way for all other books on the subject. It has become a giant in its category. This book provides a vivid exposé of the New Age movement, which the author contends is dedicated to wiping out Christianity and establishing a one world order. This movement, a vast network of occult and pagan organizations, meets the test of prophecy concerning the Antichrist.

ISBN 0-910311-03-X $8.95

To Grow By Storybook Readers by Janet Friend
Today quality of education is a major concern; consequently, more and more parents have turned to home schooling to teach their children how to read. The *To Grow By Storybook Readers* by Janet Friend can greatly enhance your home schooling reading program. The set of readers consists of 18 storybook readers plus 2 activity books. The *To Grow By Storybook Readers* has been designed to be used in conjunction with Marie LeDoux's PLAY 'N TALK phonics program but will work well with other orderly phonics programs.

These are the first phonics readers that subtly but positively instill scriptural and moral values. They're a joy to use because no prior instructional experience is necessary. The *To Grow By Storybook Readers* allows parents and children to work together learning each sound. Your child progresses through the readers and learns to appreciate his own ability to understand and think logically about word and sentence construction, thereby raising his self-esteem and confidence.

You can lead your child step-by-step into the exciting and fun world of reading and learning, without heavy reliance on memorization. Repetition and re-arrangement will leave your child begging to read page after page. Whether it's a home educational program or a phonics based program in school, these readers can substantially improve a child's reading capability and his desire to learn.

ISBN 0-910311-69-2 $44.95

The Delicate Balance by John Zajac

Did you know that the Apostle John and George Washington had revealed to them many of the same end-time events? It's true! Accomplished scientist, inventor, and speaker John Zajac asserts that science and religion are not opposed. He uses science to demonstrate the newly understood relevance of the book of Revelation. Read about the catastrophic forces at work today that the ancient prophets and others foretold. You'll wonder at George Washington's description of an angelic being which appeared to him and showed him end-time events that were to come—the accuracy of Nostradamus (who converted to Christianity)—and the warnings of St. John that are revealed in the book of Revelation—earthquakes, floods, terrorism—what does it all mean? No other author has examined these topics from Zajac's unique perspective or presented such a reasonable and concise picture of the whole.

ISBN 0-910311-57-9 $8.95

Backward Masking Unmasked by Jacob Aranza

Rock music affects millions of young people and adults with lyrics exalting drugs, Satan, violence and immorality. But there is even a more sinister threat: hidden messages that exalt the Prince of Darkness!

ISBN 0-910311-04-8 $6.95

Also on cassette tape! Hear authentic demonic backward masking from rock music.

ISBN 0-910311-23-4 $6.95

Personalities in Power: The Making of Great Leaders
by Florence Littauer

You'll laugh and cry as Florence Littauer shares with you heart-warming accounts of the personal lives of some of our greatest leaders. Learn of their triumphs and tragedies, and become aware of the different personality patterns that exist and how our leaders have been influenced by them. Discover your own strengths and weaknesses by completing the Personality Chart included in this book. *Personalities in Power* lets you understand yourself and others and helps you live up to your full potential.

ISBN 0-910311-56-0 $8.95

The Last Days Collection by Last Days Ministries

Heart-stirring, faith-challenging messages from Keith Green, David Wilkerson, Melody Green, Leonard Ravenhill, Winkie Pratney, Charles Finney and William Booth are designed to awaken complacent Christians to action.

ISBN 0-910311-42-0 $8.95

The Lucifer Connection by Joseph Carr

Shirley MacLaine and other celebrities are persuading millions that the New Age movement can fill the spiritual emptiness in their lonely lives. Joseph Carr explains why the New Age movement is the most significant and potentially destructive challenge to the church today. But is it new? How should Christians protect themselves and their children from this insidious threat? This book is a prophetic, information-packed examination by one of the most informed authors in America.

ISBN 0-910311-42-0 $7.95

Exposing the Aids Scandal: What You Don't Know Can Kill You
by Dr. Paul Cameron

Where do you turn when those who control the flow of information in this country withhold the truth? Why is the national media hiding facts from the public? Can AIDS be spread in ways we're not being told? Finally a book that gives you a total account of the AIDS epidemic, and what steps can be taken to protect yourself. What you don't know can kill you!

ISBN 0-910311-52-8 $7.95

A Reasonable Reason to Wait by Jacob Aranza

God speaks specifically about premarital sex. Aranza provides a definite, frank discussion on premarital sex. He also provides a biblical healing message for those who have already been sexually involved before marriage. This book delivers an important message for young people, as well as their parents.

ISBN 0-910311-21-8 $5.95

Jubilee on Wall Street by David Knox Barker

On October 19, 1987, the New York Stock Exchange suffered its greatest loss in history—twice that of the 1929 crash. Will this precipitate a new Great Depression? This riveting book is a look at what the author believes is the inevitable collapse of the world's economy. Using the biblical principle of the Year of Jubilee, a refreshing dose of optimism and an easy-to-read style, the author shows readers how to avoid economic devastation.

ISBN 0-933-451-03-2 $7.95

America Betrayed by Marlin Maddoux

This hard-hitting book exposes the forces in our country which seek to destroy the family, the schools and our values. This book details exactly how the news media manipulates your mind. Marlin Maddoux is the host of the popular, national radio talk show "Point of View."

ISBN 0-910311-18-8 $6.95

Devil Take the Youngest by Winkie Pratney

A history of Satan's hatred of innocence and his historical treachery against the young. Pratney begins his journey in ancient Babylon and continues through to modern-day America where infants are murdered daily and children are increasingly victimized through pornography, prostitution and humanism.

ISBN 0-910311-29-3 $8.95

Order These Books from Huntington House Publishers!

_____	America Betrayed—Marlin Maddoux — — — — —	$6.95	_____
_____	Backward Masking Unmasked—Jacob Aranza — — —	6.95	_____
_____	Deadly Deception: Freemasonry—Tom McKenney——	7.95	_____
_____	Delicate Balance—John Zajac — — — — — — —	8.95	_____
_____	Devil Take The Youngest—Winkie Pratney — — — —	8.95	_____
	The Devil's Web—Pat Pulling with Kathy Cawthon		
_____	Trade paper_____	8.95	_____
_____	Hard cover _____	16.95	_____
_____	•Dinosaurs and the Bible—Dave Unfred — — — —	12.95	_____
_____	Exposing the AIDS Scandal—Dr. Paul Cameron — —	7.95	_____
_____	From Rock to Rock—Eric Barger— — — — — —	8.95	_____
	•God's Rebels—Henry Lee Curry III, Ph.D.		
_____	Trade paper_____	12.95	_____
_____	Hard cover_____	21.95	_____
	The Hidden Dangers of the Rainbow—		
	Constance Cumbey— —	8.95	_____
_____	Inside the New Age Nightmare—Randall Baer— — —	8.95	_____
_____	Jubilee on Wall Street—David Knox Barker— — — —	7.95	_____
	•Kinsey, Sex and Fraud—Dr. Judith A. Reisman &		
_____	Edward Eichel — — — — — — —	19.95	_____
_____	Last Days Collection—Last Days Ministries — — —	8.95	_____
_____	•Lord! Why Is My Child A Rebel?—Jacob Aranza — —	6.95	_____
_____	Lucifer Connection—Joseph Carr — — — — — —	7.95	_____
	•New World Order: The Ancient Plan of Secret Societies—		
_____	William T. Still — — —	8.95	_____
_____	Personalities in Power—Florence Littauer — — — —	8.95	_____
_____	A Reasonable Reason To Wait—Jacob Aranza — — —	5.95	_____
_____	•Seduction of the Innocent Revisited—John Fulce ——	8.95	_____
	•Soft Porn Plays Hardball—Dr. Judith A. Reisman		
_____	Trade paper — — — —	8.95	_____
_____	Hard cover — — — —	16.95	_____
_____	•To Grow By Storybook Readers—Janet Friend	44.95 per set	_____
	Shipping and Handling		_____
	TOTAL		_____

•New Titles

AVAILABLE AT BOOKSTORES EVERYWHERE or order direct from:
Huntington House Publishers • P.O. Box 53788 • Lafayette, LA 70505

Send check/money order. For faster service use VISA/MASTERCARD, call
toll-free 1-800-749-4009
Add: Freight and handling, $2.00 for the first book ordered, and $.50 for each
additional book.

Enclosed is $ _____ including postage.
Card type:
VISA/MASTERCARD# _____ Exp. Date _____
Name _____
Address _____
City, State, Zipcode _____